One Hundred Sterling Years:

The Danz Family,
Sterling Theatres
and SRO

BY

Carolee Danz

WITH

David Wilma

Book Publishers Network
P.O. Box 2256
Bothell • WA • 98041
PH • 425-483-3040
www.bookpublishersnetwork.com

10 9 8 7 6 5 4 3 2 1

Printed in the United States of America

LCCN 2011903070

ISBN10 1-935359-74-6

ISBN13 978-1-935359-74-6

Editor: Julie Scandora
Cover designer: Laura Zugzda
Typographer: Stephanie Martindale

To my Dad, who has always been my rock;

To my son, who has been the light of my life;

To Logan, Blake, Devin and Mason - you are my future.

STERLING

Genuine, authentic, real, true, pure, excellent, first rate,

thoroughly excellent; a man of sterling worth

CONTENTS

ACKNOWLEDGMENTS

It's been a very long journey from the small village of Pushalot in Poland to a completed book five years later, a journey made with the companionship of and assistance from a great many people.

My editor and co-writer, David Wilma, shared his knowledge and experience to teach me the craft of turning research into a book, edited what I wrote, and added the historical context that helps bring the story alive.

My dad, Bill Danz shared memories of family and of the company, as did my uncle Fred Danz who also shared his vast knowledge of the motion picture industry and of Sterling's efforts to survive and grow through the decades.

My stepmother, Carolyn Danz remembers everything and everyone and was able to fill in a great many holes.

My sisters, Barbara Danz Daniels and Penny Danz Coe, and my brother-in-law Ted Daniels willingly shared their family memories with me.

My cousins Tad Danz, Michael Forman, Dan Appelman, JoAnn Forman Mars, and Alison Danz generously responded to multiple phone calls and endless e-mails to share information and memories and to make sure details were correct.

Zollie Volchok shared many of his wonderful memories of working in the company with John and Fred Danz and of his experiences in the world of vaudeville.

David Schooler, president of Sterling Realty Organization (SRO) spent a great many hours telling me stories of the people and projects he knew so well, literally from the ground up, and then spent more hours reading and correcting the results of those interviews.

Tom Gilchrist, vice president and treasurer of SRO, also shared his time and knowledge of the company, then read and edited the resulting tales.

The staff at Sterling Realty Organization consistently provided wonderful support. Randy Haller, company assistant controller, searched the storage room for ledgers, minute books, boxes of photographs, records, and back issues of *Spotlight*, the company newsletter. Mike Lancaster shared his thirty-eight years of knowledge at SRO, Suzette Preston provided personnel policy information. Lauren Collins scanned photos and searched out files, and Donna Riggers put up with my frequent interruptions.

My thanks go to Nicolette A. Bromberg, visual materials curator, and Blynne Kensel Olivieri, Pacific Northwest curator, and to the rest of the staff of the University of Washington Libraries Special Collections, the repository of the Sterling records, for their patience and continuous assistance as I delved through the thirty-eight boxes of Sterling papers and roamed through the Polk Directories over and over again.

Many thanks go to:

Leonard Garfield, executive director; Lorraine McConaghy, historian, and Carolyn Marr, librarian at the Museum of History and Industry for sharing photographs, interviews, and information with me.

David Favaloro, director of curatorial affairs for the Lower East Side Tenement Museum in New York for sharing photographs and providing a special visit to an apartment my family might have lived in during the early 1890s.

Patricia Eastham, who purchased the Narada Apartments from Jessie Danz and lives in the apartment the Danzes once occupied, for allowing me to visit and to photograph the apartment and the view from the top of Queen Anne Hill.

Julia Drebin and Nora Leech for their excellent research assistance.

Russ Knudsen for gathering memoirs from the "John Danz/Bel-Vue Theater Alumni" and the "Factoria Cinemas Alumni" Facebook groups.

Tobias Coughlin-Bogue for his patient editing of the content, grammar, and punctuation of each chapter.

Shelly Shapiro for being my outside set of eyes and for giving her insightful comments.

To my family for patiently putting up with my frequent responses to their invitations of "Sorry, but I must stay focused."

And to my son, Jason Horning, for his constant support throughout, for reading and editing the final version, and for his generous response. He said, "In the words of Fred Danz, 'It is good.'"

FOREWORD

The story of John Danz and SRO is a classic, not just the arduous journey from the Pale of Settlement in Russia and the success of hard-working and visionary immigrants, but the birth and growth of American popular culture witnessed by "going to the movies." But much of the history of the motion-picture industry is written from Hollywood from the point of view of the producers, the directors, and the stars. Countless books and documentaries, even the feature films themselves, try to capture what it was like to make movies. From the bandit in *The Great Train Robbery* of 1903 firing his revolver at the audience to the computer graphics of *Avatar*, fans want answers to that natural question, "How did they do that?" Hollywood tells its own compelling stories of artists and technology coming together, not just to generate revenue but to create a new art form. This art form took hold and took over the national consciousness until references to the movies could be found everywhere. Movie-goers went home, not just entertained but changed in some way. Almost nothing in our culture today hasn't been, in some way, influenced by the motion-picture camera and the phonograph.

But what about where incandescent light actually met eyeballs, where America lined up every night and many afternoons to pay a quarter for half a pasteboard ticket and ninety minutes in another world? What was involved in actually delivering this world-changing product to people who kept coming back for more?

John Danz sold shirts, jackets, and trousers in Seattle's Pioneer Square area, the roughest and meanest neighborhood north of San Francisco, when he opened a nickelodeon next door. The theater was probably little more than benches set before a white sheet with a hand-operated projector in the back. Five cents bought about twenty minutes of comedy, drama, and travel.

John was not satisfied just to collect nickels and dimes and hire someone to run a projector. He knew he had to compete with other exhibitors who enjoyed sweetheart deals with distributors. He added organ and piano music to the silent reels. As John opened more theaters, he needed help, particularly in keeping tabs on daily operations. He employed his sons, Bill and Fred, and his son-in-law. Others joined John's team, some for a short time, some for many years. "The boys" learned the business and tried their best to meet John's high expectations of performance. No detail of a movie house escaped attention from a pair of dirty hands or frayed collar to the apparently universal issue of restroom deodorant cakes. The staffs of Sterling's theaters worked hard to deliver a high-quality experience for movie viewers, and thousands of young people had their first work experience measuring up to an exacting set of standards.

John's son Fred entered the theater business as an eleven-year-old ticket-taker and usher and dropped out of college because he thought he could learn more from his father than from the professors. Fred influenced the business perhaps even more than John, the founder, and was both his father's son and his own man. First-hand accounts of Fred show an interesting guy who maintained the traditions of long hours and meticulous attention to high quality for theater patrons and expected no less from every member of his organization. At one point the business employed 2,000 people. One manager describes Fred's reputation as "fearsome," but a young employee could still meet with Fred personally and pitch an idea. The young man's idea was ahead of its time, but Fred treated him with respect, an attitude expected of everyone in the company. Fred was not just a manager; he was a leader.

Fred was part of the generation that fueled Seattle's economic and cultural growth beginning in the 1950s. Not only was he active and creative in business, but he also threw his energy behind cultural, educational, and charitable initiatives that transformed the Seattle area into one of the most livable in the nation.

When people learn that I am a writer, they always ask about my current project. When I was working on the history of Seattle Children's Hospital ("The Orthopedic" to old-timers), just about everyone had some connection with that amazing institution; they or a child or a parent had been treated there. When I mention Sterling Recreation Organization and the Danz theaters, I get similar responses. My own brother-in-law worked for a time in a Sterling bowling center, and his friends worked in the theaters. I currently live a few blocks from the Oak Tree Cinema, one of the company's last new theater constructions. On the social networking Web site Facebook, a former Sterling staffer has organized fan pages around a couple of the old Sterling theaters. The posts reflect a genuine affection for the memories of Sterling Theatres.

My own memories include that of SRO's Magnolia Theatre the closest movie house after I moved to Seattle in 1966. There is also the Northgate Theatre. In 1974, I was a federal narcotics agent, recovering from some pretty serious injuries caused when my car rolled during a chase up on the Canadian border. Several weeks after leaving two hospitals, I was ready to venture out. My wife and I went to see *Blazing Saddles* starring Mel Brooks. Free health tip: If you are recovering from six broken ribs and a collapsed lung, don't go to an uproariously funny movie.

Sterling and its leaders have demonstrated a remarkable flexibility and nimbleness when it comes to finding the right fit in business. Bowling lanes proved a profitable way to convert a poorly-performing movie house to a new use. Bowling centers became a great way to add to the draw of the movies. Drive-ins, vacant and unused during the day, became swap meets. When video tapes hit the market and fans could take their movies home, Sterling was one of the first to embrace the technology and the business. The variety of Sterling businesses over the years is amazing.

But big is not always better at Sterling. At the point where the company reached more than a hundred screens and hundreds of bowling lanes, Fred guided the company through reinventing itself in commercial real estate. Although John Danz ran entertainment businesses, his Sterling Men's Wear was incorporated to invest in real estate so Fred and Sterling have, in a way, fulfilled the master plan of the founder.

One other thing has endured in the company's history, an absolute insistence on an exceptional product. The company's reputation was in the cheery face and freshly pressed uniform of every theater usher and property manager. The character of Sterling is today reflected not just in the quality of its properties but also in the foresight of the family owners who continue to plan for the future.

David Wilma
December 2010

INTRODUCTION

I am a frequent voyager. One of my remarkable journeys was a land trip to the Baltic countries in June of 2006. I was in Lithuania when one of the couples in the group invited me to join them on a separate visit to their ancestral village. We spent the day in and around the small village of Pushalot (POO-sha-lot) an hour or two out of Vilna, where we slowly wandered around the town, learning how to identify which houses had once been Jewish homes, visiting the town square, the old synagogue (now a saltpeter factory), and the Jewish cemetery. My friends were very moved by the experience as they imagined their grandparents walking the very cobbles upon which we tread.

My name is Carolee Danz. I am the daughter of William Frank Danz and Selma Goldstein Danz (Vinmont), granddaughter of John and Jessie Danz, the great-granddaughter of Louis and Hannah Danowsky and Maurice and Annie Mohr and the great-great-granddaughter of Owsiej and Fredja Suransky. I am also the mother of Jason Earl Horning and the grandmother of Logan, Blake, Devin, and Mason Horning.

As a voyager, I travel somewhere in the world as often as possible, trying to see, experience, and learn as much as I can before my energy gives out and I am no longer able to manage the eco-expedition trips

I enjoy. On the visit to Pushalot, I found myself thinking that some of my own relatives most likely came from similar small villages, and then I began to wonder where they were from and what their lives were like. I had already begun researching the history of the Sterling Realty Organization, but this experience changed the project into one that would include the history of the family. That was the beginning for me. When I got home, I registered with Ancestry.com and began researching my family history.

In 2005, I was getting ready to retire from my position with our family company, Sterling Realty Organization, when David Schooler, the president of the company asked me if I would be willing to write the one-hundred-year history of the company. The 100th anniversary was coming up sometime in the next several years, although at that time, no one was sure exactly when the company had begun. When I agreed to do the research, I began a fascinating journey into the history of the company and my ancestral past as well.

Now I had to learn how to write a book. Where to start? I started by interviewing my uncle, Fred Danz, one of the sons of the founder of the company, John Danz. I was immensely fortunate to be able to complete most of my interviews with Fred before he passed away in mid-2009. My father, John's eldest son, had already lost most of his memory, but he was able to identify some of the family members in the photos included in this book.

I spent many hours each week at the University of Washington in the Special Collections archives where all the oldest preserved records of Sterling Theatres are located — all thirty-eight boxes. I visited the library at the Museum of History and Industry several times, inspecting photos and other records, and I spent time in the Washington State Archives located at Bellevue College to search for photos of the homes and places of business once occupied by my family.

I searched through boxes and boxes in the storage room at the company's offices, interviewed long-time employees, delved into minute books and accounting ledgers from more than a dozen companies, scanned hundreds of photographs, and put together a massive timeline covering the ten decades of Sterling Theaters, Sterling Recreation, and Sterling Realty.

In 2008, I took another journey, this time to several of the towns and cities that at least six of my ancestors had come from. I started with an extensive tour of Romania. I can still remember my great-grandmother Clara Goldstein who always said she was Romanian. I ended the Romanian visit with a week in Chisinau, Moldova. Grandma Goldstein and her husband, Hyman, had lived and married in what she called Kishinev in 1880 when she was sixteen years old, and they soon emigrated to the United States, arriving in 1882.

My mother's great-grandfather Simon Hochfeld arrived from Kishinev in 1888 at the age of thirty-one, bringing with him a family bible in which is listed (in Hebrew) many generations of my male ancestors, men who were rabbis through the centuries throughout Europe, all the way back to Akiva of Thessaloniki in Greece, having fled there from Spain during the Spanish Inquisition.

From Moldova, I went back to Lithuania and paid a brief visit to Wladyslawow, where my great-great-grandfather Owsiej Suransky came from (it was part of Poland when he lived there), and then to Suwalki in Poland, where his wife's family, Frejdy Leibowny Postawelska Suransky's relatives lived for many generations. In each of these places, including Rumania and Moldova, I was hosted by local Jewish community organizations and visited whatever Jewish sights were available: old synagogues, residential areas, schools, and in each town, the historic Jewish cemeteries, or what was left of them.

From Suwalki, I went back to Warsaw where Louis Danowsky was born. I had been to Warsaw on the first journey to Poland, before I knew I had relatives from there, and had visited the old and new Jewish sights and learned much of the history of the community. On this second visit to Warsaw, I became more familiar with the city and with the history of the community, although I have not been able to find any traces of my relatives to date. Almost all traces of Warsaw's Jews were erased in the Holocaust.

Soon after I returned home, I started writing, editing, rewriting, rewriting, and rewriting. Fortunately, I was put in touch with David

Wilma who agreed to edit for me and just happened to be a talented historian and author who was willing to add his expertise to create the historical framework for the story.

What follows is the result of my five-year project. I hope this story will be as interesting for you as it was for me. I was fascinated by each new discovery, each new relationship unearthed, and each new factoid.

Carolee Danz
January 2011

The Immigrants

❧ The Danz Family ❧

Louis Danowsky, the immigrant ancestor of the Danz family, hailed from Warsaw, Poland, part of the Russian empire. His eldest brother, Hyman Lizer Danowsky, was born in 1832 and was already nineteen when Louis was born. A third son died as a young man. I have not yet discovered anything about Louis's parents.

Under czarist rule, one son of each family was required to register for conscription into the army. Hyman never registered so Louis went into the service in his stead. He would have been eighteen in September 1869. At that time, all conscripts served for twenty-five years. Most were between the ages of eighteen and thirty-five, but Jews could be conscripted as young as twelve. In 1874, Czar Alexander II, who had already freed Russian serfs from lifelong servitude, reduced the compulsory military duty to six years. Under the new law, Louis probably left the army sometime in 1875. In 1877, at the age of twenty-six, he married Hannah, whose maiden name I have not learned. I have been told that Hannah was born in Minsk, in present-day Belarus, in November 1863 and that she had a stepfather and a half-sister, but I have yet to find any other information about her. When Hannah and Louis married, she was thirteen or fourteen years old, twelve years his junior. Louis was a very tall man, over six feet, when the average height of a man was about five feet five inches. In family photos, Hannah appears to be tall as well, just a few inches shorter than Louis.

The precise reasons for the Danowsky family moving east from Warsaw are unknown. Bryansk was a regional trading center with factories manufacturing cannon and ammunition for the czar's army and navy. Perhaps, like so many soldiers through the centuries, Bryansk was simply where Louis found himself a civilian again.

The Danowskys lived in Bryansk when their first child, Israel, was born in September of 1877. Israel grew up to become the man we know as John Danz. A second son, Silas, may have been born in 1879, but died in infancy. Simon arrived in 1881.

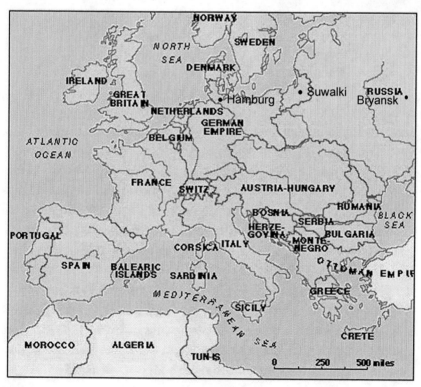

Bryansk, Russia

The Danowskys, however, would soon leave Bryansk. Imperial policies against Jews were undoubtedly a major factor in Louis and Hannah's migration. The czars and their nobles felt threatened by the growing economic influence of Jews and imposed discriminatory laws, hoping the Jews would emigrate. Jews could not own property. They could only live within the Pale of Settlement, a designated region of western Russia, generally outside of cities. This permanent condition of oppression intensified feelings of culture, family, and community among Jews and kept them distinct and separated from the rest of Russian society.

There are several different stories regarding what caused the family to leave Russia. Their departure coincided with the beginning of a particularly vicious round of pogroms — officially sanctioned riots against Jews. Family lore holds that Louis ran a tavern in Bryansk, an activity forbidden to Jews, so he registered the business in the name of one of the Russian barmaids. Perhaps, during the pogroms, she saw an opportunity for profit and reported Louis to the czarist authorities. Whatever the story, Louis had ample reason to flee Russia with his family.

John Danz liked to tell the story of being "thrown out of Russia." As the family reached the ditch that marked the border between Russia and the Prussian empire, Louis and Hannah picked up each of their children and handed them across. Given the problems facing them in Russia, tossing their children across a ditch seems quite reasonable. In his later years, John was fond of making the incident a bit of immigrant humor.

I have yet to locate a steamship passenger list with the Danowsky family on it, but I did find John's naturalization papers. In his affidavit for United States citizenship, he says the family made their way to Germany and sailed from Hamburg for the United States. This was the usual route for Jews fleeing oppression from this part of the world. Hannah told her children in later years how sick the family was on the passage across the ocean. Immigrants had become big business by the 1880s, and ship owners crammed as many poor refugees into steerage as the ships would handle. Safety and comfort were afterthoughts. We can only imagine the conditions deep in the hold where hundreds of individuals ate, vomited, moaned, toileted, slept, and endured for three weeks or more. Sitting on deck provided some relief from the disgusting conditions below, but there passengers had to endure the cold wind of the north Atlantic. Immigrants were probably afforded fewer comforts than cattle. Shippers were paid only for live cattle delivered. Immigrants paid their fares up front and arrival alive was optional.

I don't know where the Danowskys entered the U.S. (New York and Baltimore were important debarkation ports for the Hamburg-America Line), but the family's first home in the new country was in St. Louis, Missouri, in 1882. Wherever and whenever they landed, when they reached St. Louis, they were likely to have been welcomed and assisted by the Hebrew Immigrant Aid Society, which still operates today, or by the Hebrew Benevolent Society, founded in 1842 and now known as Jewish Family Services. These organizations helped resettle Jews from Eastern Europe by arranging housing, establishing connections with the Jewish community, finding jobs, and helping immigrants learn the basics of living in America.

Louis became a peddler, selling kitchen and household supplies to rural farms and households. In the 1880s, the majority of America still lived on the land, far from towns with any sort of commercial services. Peddlers in carts and wagons visited isolated homesteads on the prairie, selling everything from pots and pans to spices, clothing, and farm tools. Travelers over the crude roads sank deep into the mud in the winter (unless frozen) and choked on dust in the summer. The advent of mail-order catalogs and the Railway Express Agency eventually cut into door-to-door work, but Louis pursued this occupation in Missouri, Kansas, and later, Oregon.

A baby girl, name unknown, was born in St. Louis in 1882 but died in infancy. Infant mortality remained high in the new country, particularly among poor immigrants. Daughter Sarah was born on December 25, 1884. Louis's travels gave him an opportunity to examine a new land that may have seemed to him not unlike Poland and Russia. For the poor of any nation, the opportunity to own a piece of land in a new country represented a dream come true. The transcontinental railroad companies, with vast tracts of land granted to them by the U.S. government, advertised extensively in Europe to attract settlers. Louis found some available land, and the family left St. Louis about the spring of 1885, settling on a homestead near Liberal, Kansas, a new town just beginning to grow. Pursuant to the law signed by Abraham Lincoln, a farmer could file a claim on 160 acres of land. If Louis improved it and lived on it five years, "proving up," he could file for title and own it outright. Unfortunately, this was a time of drought. Louis, Hannah, and the children endured two harsh winters and at least one dry summer, living in a sod hut, but like so many other homesteaders, they were unable to make a go of it. Another son, Joseph, was born in January 1887 on the homestead in Liberal.

Louis left Kansas around 1887 with ten-year-old Israel next to him on the peddler's wagon. Israel had attended school in St. Louis and then in Kansas, but when they moved this time, he dropped out. John told his grandchildren that he had a formal education only through the fourth grade, but as we got older, we realized that he was thoroughly educated. Louis and John turned the team west, carrying all the household goods toward Oregon, which had represented the promise of a new life in the American West since the 1830s. The lush Willamette Valley supported pastures, orchards, and crops that were channeled to the outside world via Portland and the Columbia River. Once transcontinental railroads connected the coasts, migrants surged west.

Hannah and the younger children followed Louis and Israel to their new home in the West by train. Railroad companies offered bargain fares to migrants who would populate the West, as they would likely be customers again in the future. The migrant coaches, sometimes called Zulu Cars, were far more comfortable than steerage, but still pretty spare. Passengers sat and slept on hard seats, often just a bench against the wall. Their meals came from what they could pack or from vendors who worked the stations and the trains.

One family researcher says Louis first found a new home for the family in 1888 in Wallula, on the Columbia River near Walla Walla, Washington. This makes some sense, given that overland migrants to Oregon traveled the last few hundred miles on the Snake and Columbia Rivers by steamer and Louis may have been attracted by stories of opportunity in the river town. By 1889, they were living in Portland on Front Street where daughter Lillian was born on December 14, 1889. Another daughter, Eva, was born in Portland in December of 1893. By 1900, the family had moved to Oregon City, outside of Portland, where their last child, daughter Pearl, was born in 1901.

My maternal great-grandparents, Hyman and Clara Goldstein, joined the Danowsky family in Oregon. The Danowskys and the Goldsteins may even have known each other, either in Kansas or the immigrant community in St. Louis. They certainly knew each other in Oregon. My maternal grandfather, Moe Goldstein Bernhard (born in 1892 in Oregon City) remembered his mother saying, "Let's go visit the Danowskys."

Louis continued to work as a peddler for a time, with young Israel alongside him, learning the art of the sale. At this point, sources disagree about where and how they worked. One source says Louis continued to work as a peddler, traveling from farm to farm, selling hardware items. Others think Louis exchanged the wagon for something more stationary and opened a men's clothing store or even several clothing stores in The Dalles, Portland, and Astoria. All would have been easily reached by river steamer. Given Louis's history as a peddler, these stores would probably have been individual enterprises rather than any sort of chain. I can easily imagine Louis and his sons setting up shop in rented space for a time and then moving on.

The Panic of 1893 slowed things for several years. It was the largest and deepest economic recession in United States history and would remain so until 1929. Capitalists and corporations found themselves bankrupt, sources of money dried up, and many Americans reverted to a barter economy. Tens of thousands of working men and women found themselves without jobs and worse, without prospect of anything soon. These were the days before unemployment

Danz Family 1890: Si, John, and Anna in back row. Sarah, Louis, infant Lilly, Joe in front.

benefits. Although I have no direct information, I can conclude that the Danowskys experienced some lean years as their customers stopped coming in for new clothes.

Louis and Israel eventually found a home for the family in Portland. The family is listed in the Portland Polk City Directory in 1898 at 191 Lincoln Street as Louis (occupation: peddler), Samuel (I have no idea who Samuel is unless Israel was trying out American sounding names), and Simon. Wives were not listed in the directory until later. The family drops out of the Portland directory until 1903, when Simon Dans reappears by himself, living at 293½ First Street. City directories were fairly complete listings of residents so it's reasonable to assume that Louis took his family to other communities to do business.

Sometime during these years, Israel struck out on his own. He worked as a newsboy in Oregon, as a Western Union messenger in San Francisco, and as a cowhand on ranches in Nevada. He also worked the wheat harvest in the Wallula area for a summer or two.

❦ ❧

The economic turnaround in the country started slowly in 1895 as reports of gold strikes in Alaska and the Klondike attracted prospectors, just as California's gold rush did in 1849. Ambitious men, and a few women, booked passage on ships leaving Puget Sound for Alaska, providing the region with much-needed business. In 1897, Seattle newspapers celebrated the arrival of the SS *Portland* and its passengers carrying "a ton of gold" from the Klondike. The story spread across the country, and thousands more headed west and then north to strike it rich. The rush of miners became a flood, and Seattle was ideally positioned to profit. Miners hoping to prospect in the Klondike, a Canadian territory, were each required to demonstrate that they had a year's worth of provisions before they were admitted with Northwest Mounted Policemen at border posts ensuring compliance. Seattle's merchants happily outfitted the ambitious travelers and offered buyer's guides with recommended purchases. When some adventurers returned with their pockets full of gold dust, the merchants took another taste. Seattle led the nation's recovery from the Panic. Then, in 1899, the U.S. became a world power by defeating Spain in a short war. Congress annexed the Philippines and other Spanish territories. Trade with the Orient blossomed, and Seattle's prosperity continued to grow.

Not everyone migrating west sought to strike it rich. Tens of thousands more surged into the region to take up land or sign up for jobs in extraction industries, such as logging, fishing, mining, and processing logs, fish, and ore. Every Saturday, men lined up for their pay envelopes. Mills on Puget Sound often paid their people in scrip, redeemable only at a bank, or at the company offices in Seattle. Millworkers from Bainbridge Island to Camano Island took "mosquito fleet" steamers to Seattle to cash in their vouchers. From the paymaster's windows, the workers repaired back to their homes and families or, more commonly, to the fleshpots and gambling dens "below the line" of Yesler Way.

In 1903, the Danowskys boarded a train to Seattle. Louis and Israel—now going by John—saw what others saw. There was money to be made on Elliott Bay. The family appears for the first time in a 1904 Seattle city directory as Dans. Jews frequently anglicized their surnames to circumvent anti-Semitism or simply to make their names sound more American. Once again, there are various versions of how the name became Danz. Fred, John's second son, told me that John wanted to change his name to Davis, but there was already a real estate man named John Davis in Seattle. Thus, John changed the name to Dans. Another tale claims that John then thought the name looked better with the sweep of the "z" at the end. John Danz, formerly Israel Danowsky, would have been about twenty-six years old.

The Danz family's first home in Seattle was at 1502 Terry Avenue, at Pike Street. They lived there only for about a year. From late 1904 or early 1905 until sometime in 1908, they lived where Harborview Hospital is now located, at 814 Alder Street. From 1908 to 1910, they were in the Central Area at 218 28th Avenue South at Jackson Street.

When they moved to Seattle, Louis sent for his nephew to join the family in Seattle. Julius Labe (Yudel Labe) Danowsky was the son of Louis's elder brother, Hyman Lizer. Julius was born in 1852, so he was almost the same age as his uncle Louis. (I assume Hyman had died as Julius came to Seattle with his mother, Gittle Whitesman Danowsky.) Louis also sponsored Isaac Pass, who was married to his niece, Rose. Rose joined her husband, Isaac, with their five children in 1907. Julius and Isaac both established dairy farms in the Wilburton area of Bellevue.

In 1903, Louis opened a clothing store in Seattle at 208 Second Avenue South. The next year he had two stores, one at 203 Occidental and another at 202 Main Street. In the Polk Directory during these years, John was listed as a clerk at the L. Danz and Son (singular) clothing store. Soon Simon and then Joseph are shown as working for L. Danz and Sons. The locations of the stores changed often, but the name remained.

I found conflicting information about the clothing stores. The name L. Danz and Sons leads me to believe that Louis and his sons owned the stores jointly, although this was probably not a formalized business relationship. Soon Louis was happy to pursue other fields and leave the operation of the stores to his sons. Louis opened a shoe repair shop in 1905 and tried being a shoemaker in 1907, but this lasted only about a year. (The year 1907 was another time of economic contraction in the country.) In 1909, he identified himself as a tailor in the directory. In 1911, when John opened a store entirely separate from his father and brothers, Louis returned to operate his own clothing store, which had moved again, to 211 Occidental. He continued to operate the Occidental store until sometime in 1917.

It seems to me that the businessmen of the family tried their luck at one rented location for a few years and moved on to another as conditions changed and new opportunities presented themselves. Traffic patterns in Seattle shifted as streets south of Yesler Way were realigned with the streets to the north. Some of the streets on Seattle's steeper hills were regraded. In 1906, when King Street Station opened at Second Avenue South and South King Street to provide a terminal for both the Great Northern Railway and Northern Pacific Railroad, newly arrived travelers hit city streets from a new direction. Union

Station opened at Fourth Avenue South and South Jackson Street in 1911. Modern structures, like the Lowman Building (built in 1906) at First Avenue and Cherry Street, changed the character of their neighborhoods as well as that of the retail scene. When Louis first came west in 1887, he changed cities as the needs arose. In Seattle, he did the same, but with addresses instead.

In 1909, at about the age of thirty-one, John moved into a place of his own. Louis and Hannah and the other children, now adults, moved four more times before settling in 1917 into a home at 161 27th Avenue. Hannah died in 1925, having lived in that home to the end. She was sixty-one years old. Louis continued to live in the house until his death in 1944. My father, Bill Danz, remembers his grandfather Louis roofing his own home in his nineties. He was still hale and hardy but went downhill quickly thereafter and died at the age of ninety-two.

Home of Louis and Anna Danz, 1917—1944.
(Washington State Archives.)

Louis's son John was of much shorter stature than his father, perhaps five feet four inches. In a wedding photo of John and Jessie they appear to be almost the same height.

❧ The Mohr-Suransky Family ❧

Jessie (Mohr) Danz's father came from the province of Herzegovina, in the Austrian Empire. Family tradition holds that Maurice Mohr, who was born Maurice Mord in 1861, came to New York in 1879 at the age of eighteen. In that year, immigrants landed at Castle Garden Emigrant Landing Depot at the tip of Manhattan. Anywhere from eight million to twelve million immigrants entered the U.S. there between 1855 and 1892. After that, Ellis Island became the entry point for New York.

Maurice was the son of Gerson Mord and Elka Sachsenhaus Mord, but I don't have any other information about him other than the 1910 Census return, which says he was born in Austria and immigrated in 1886. This contradicts the family story of his arrival in 1879. In 1886, he would have been about twenty-five years old. There is a Morris Mord listed in the Staten Island City Directory of 1890, occupation "dry goods," at 132 Broad Street near the Verrazano Narrows. While we know that in the new country he changed his name to Mohr, the 1887 marriage certificate of Morris and Annie Suransky shows his name is still Mord.

Annie Suransky's family came from Wladyslawow and Suwalki in the Russian Empire. Wladyslawow was a very small town in northeastern Poland. It is still a small town but is now in Lithuania. Suwalki was a larger city with industry and an active mercantile life. In 1842, there was a population of perhaps 10,000. That year, Owsiej (roughly pronounced OV-shay) Suransky of Wladyslawow married Frejdy Leibowny Postawelska of Suwalki when he was twenty and she was nineteen. They had eight children, the seventh child being Annie, born in 1864 in Suwalki.

Annie immigrated to New York in 1876 when she was just twelve years old, probably following the other refugees from Russia through Hamburg. My great-aunt Jennie Mohr said that Annie crossed the

Frejdy Suransky and daughter Leah, ca. 1870-1880, Poland.

Levine kitchen at 97 Orchard Street, New York. Photo by Battman Studios, Courtesy Lower East Side Tenement Museum.

Atlantic from Suwalki in steerage, by herself, to join an aunt. This aunt was most likely Mrs. Bella Altkrug, of 17 Barrett Street in Brooklyn, who might have been a sister of Frejdy. Bella's name was found in the address book of one of the cousins who also emigrated from Poland around the same time. My grandmother, Jessie, told me that Annie was treated very poorly by this aunt, as if she were a slave. Like so many other immigrant women, Annie found a job in a sweatshop, sewing clothing with long hours, dreadful conditions, and pitiful pay.

In 1883, Owsiej died in Suwalki. Annie's mother, Frejdy, left Poland in 1888 with two of her grown children for New York. In June 1890 the three of them lived together in a tenement apartment at 97 Orchard Street on Manhattan's Lower East Side. Tenements were multi-story apartment buildings with single entrances and no elevators. In the nineteenth century, they were typically overcrowded, uncomfortable, unsafe, and unsanitary. Even so, landlords were able to extract exorbitant rents from immigrants who had no other options. The building at 97 Orchard Street is now the Tenement Museum. In the roster of residents, Annie's family is mistakenly listed as Fannie, Jacob, and Yetta *Suralski*. When Fannie (Frejdy) died of a heart ailment on December 7, 1893, at the age of seventy, her death certificate listed her as living in that same building. She was laid to rest in the Congregation Rodeph Shalom section (section 30) of Union Fields Cemetery in Ridgewood, Queens.

Twenty-three-year-old Annie Suransky met tall, handsome Maurice Mord and married him in 1887. They most likely met because they lived in the same building at 364 East 71 Street in New York. He was twenty-six and it appears he had been in the country for only, perhaps, a year. Maurice was a bit of a rake, with a great smile and dancing eyes. Annie and Maurice stayed in New York for a few years, where three daughters were born: Lillian in January 1888, my grandmother Jessie, born on Staten Island in February 1889, and Jennie, born in New York in 1892. The family spent time in Pennsylvania then moved on to California at about the time of the Panic of 1893. Freda was born there in 1894, and George, the only son, was born in Los Angeles in 1895.

Tenement Museum, 97 Orchard Street, New York Photo by Keiko Niwa, Courtesy Lower East Side Tenement Museum.

Maurice Mohr family, San Francisco, ca. 1895 , back row Maurice and Annie, second row Unknown, Freda, George, Unknown, front row Lillie, Jennie (died 1901), Jessie.

Maurice dragged the family back and forth across the country several times. Perhaps following stories of easy wealth, he moved his brood to Seattle where Esther was born in November of 1898. In 1899, the Mords—two adults, four daughters and a son—lived at 715 Main Street, in today's International District. Maurice worked as a traveling salesman of dry goods and was gone from home much of the time. When he was home, he preferred the society of saloons, which were plentiful in Seattle. His daughters dragged him home inebriated many, many times. The family then moved east again to Pottsville, Pennsylvania where, sadly, daughter Jennie died in 1901. They were back in Seattle in 1903.

Maurice didn't think it was important for his daughters to continue in school or go to college. Few women of the early 1900s went to college. He expected them to work to help pay for their brother George's college education. In 1905, Lillie and Jessie found positions as stenographers at John F. Reed, 2707 Second Avenue, in today's Belltown. The next year, Jessie worked at Kelly-Clarke Co., an import-export business that also distributed items like fruit and salmon. In 1907, she moved on to Stetson & Post Lumber Co. at 522 24th Avenue South, just south of King Street, where she remained until her marriage in 1911.

By 1909, Maurice and Annie were back in Pennsylvania, where the youngest child, also named Jennie, was born. My great-aunt Jennie was always annoyed that she had been named after the first Jennie who died in 1901. It was not unusual for families to name a child after an older, deceased sibling as a sort of memorial, but Aunt Jennie resented it.

During these years, the other three sisters started working; Freda also became a stenographer while Esther worked as a seamstress, and Jennie taught piano. Freda, Esther, and Jennie all still felt strongly about attending college, and Annie agreed. Annie colluded with them and kept the either absent or drunk Maurice from knowing that they were going to school.

All the Mord girls put their educations to good use. I have been told that Freda was the first woman in Washington State to receive

Maurice and
Annie Mohr,
ca. 1910.

The Mohr children, ca. 1910, left to right, Jennie, Esther,
George, Freda, Jessie and Lillie (UW Special Collections).

a degree in social work, but so far have not been able to confirm the information. She moved to Los Angeles to join her sister Lillie and eventually became the executive director of Jewish Family Services in Los Angeles. Esther became the president of Sarah Lawrence College. Jennie became a concert-level pianist and also trained as a mathematician. She worked at Harvard on the Big Bang Theory and eventually became a professor of Social Work at Simmons College near Boston. With financial support from his sisters, George attended the University of Washington and then medical school. He studied with Sigmund Freud in Vienna and eventually headed the child psychiatry department at Cedars-Sinai Hospital in Los Angeles.

The Haberdasher

❧ 1911–1920 ❧

By 1911, Seattle had just finished thirty years of phenomenal growth. The population grew more than tenfold in the 1880s. In the 1890s, despite the Great Fire of 1889, which leveled downtown, the Panic of 1893, which plunged the nation into a depression, and the exodus of half the residents from both disasters, the population still doubled. From 1900 to 1910, the number of residents tripled. The new arrivals crossed prairies and mountains, not behind teams of oxen but in railroad coaches, turning what used to be a six-month journey into one of only a few days. The city and the region swelled with people speaking a multitude of languages, anxious to wrest their share of economic opportunity from the new land. City boundaries ballooned north, south, and west to absorb West Seattle and Ballard. New neighborhoods like Columbia City, Green Lake, and Queen Anne Hill grew with the extension of streetcar lines, often built by developers hoping to lure lot buyers.

Seattle businessmen prospered as the wealth of the interior rode in on rails and trade from the Orient and Alaska flowed into Seattle's waterfront to stimulate business even more. No fewer than four transcontinental rail lines served the city.

With the economic boom came the growth of civic culture. A symphony orchestra, a fine arts society (later the Seattle Arts Museum), exciting new academic departments at the University of Washington (Marine Sciences, Far East Studies, Forestry), Children's Orthopedic Hospital (later Seattle Children's Hospital), Seattle City Light, beautiful Carnegie libraries downtown and in the neighborhoods, public works projects like the Duwamish Waterway and the Lake Washington Ship Canal, and many other institutions formed the backbone and brawny arms and legs of the young city. To celebrate progress, civic leaders staged a world's fair in 1909, the Alaska-Yukon-Pacific Exposition.

Seattle boasted another, less genteel, aspect to its economy. To better serve—and fleece—miners, loggers, fishermen, sailors, farm workers, and other consumers of gambling, alcohol, and more carnal entertainments, the city fathers had established a "restricted area" south of Yesler Way. As long as the gamblers, procurers, and working girls kept their businesses "below the line," they could ply their trades and prosper. The arrangement became so institutionalized that the police chief levied a tax on games and girls, dutifully collected by Seattle's Finest in full uniform. The issue of an "open" or "closed" city became pivotal to the outcome of municipal elections. In 1910, when the mayor of Seattle, Hiram Gill, granted a license to build the world's largest brothel across the right of way for a city street, voters, their numbers swelled by newly enfranchised women, sent him packing. (The building and its hundreds of tiny rooms remained there until the 1940s when a Boeing bomber crashed into it and destroyed it.)

Photos of the 1900s show a skyline with a perpetual smudge from thousands of coal-fired stoves, furnaces, and boilers. Forests of utility poles and wires beyond number jockeyed for space along streets and alleys. Horse-drawn wagons, carriages, and pedestrians dodged streetcars. Exposed tracks threatened to trip or ensnare the careless and unlucky. On the waterfront, railroad passengers had to make their way across seven sets of railroad tracks to the frame shelter serving as a passenger depot. Although electric lighting had caught on in the business district, neighborhood residents still squinted under kerosene lamps until the competing utility companies could run wires out their way. Unseen and un-smelled in old photographs, raw sewage went to back yard privies or washed directly into Elliott Bay. Thousands of horses and sputtering automobiles added their discharges to the stench of the city at the turn of the young twentieth century.

Among the immigrant groups that contributed depth and color to Seattle were newly arrived Russian Jews. The population of Russian Jews was around 1,000 in 1905. Within a year, a Jewish newspaper and a Jewish settlement house sprang up to serve the refugees fleeing persecution and worse at the hands of the czar. Added to the mix were Sephardic Jews from the Mediterranean lands of a crumbling Ottoman Empire.

In the 1900s, the opportunities for a men's clothier showed promise. Seasonal workers from farms, logging camps, and fishing boats spent the winter months in Seattle. Often they returned to town with the same clothes they had worn when they had left months before. With their meager wages, they usually invested in a bath, a shave, and a haircut. The next order of business was often something new and clean to wear.

I found clothing stores listed under John's name as early as 1909. He might have owned these stores with his father and brothers and sold his interest to go out on his own before he married. In the earlier years, the stores are listed as L. Danz Clothing. After 1910, the stores at 206 Main and 119 Yesler are still listed as L. Danz stores and under Louis's name. But after 1910, we find J. Danz stores listed separately.

At some point during these years John noticed a young woman on the Yesler Way trolley on her way to work. As was proper in those days, he arranged to be introduced. Many years later, Jessie told a reporter that she thought John was a very handsome young man and she was pleased when he came on his bicycle to court her, played his mandolin for her, and took her for canoe rides around Seward Park. The fact that he was eleven years her senior did not dampen the attraction.

Jessie and John Danz were married on March 19, 1911, just a few weeks after John opened what I mark as his first clothing store. They exchanged vows in the living room of Jessie's home with about 100 people in attendance. Rabbi Samuel Koch of Temple de Hirsh officiated with Jessie's eldest sister, Lillie, and Lillie's husband, Julius

Jessie Mohr and John Danz wedding photo, 1911.

Jessie Mohr, John Danz, J.J. Friedman standing, Lillie Mohr seated, 1911.

Joseph (Joe) Friedman, as their official witnesses. Jessie and John began their married lives in John's apartment on James Street at Ninth Avenue. Just three months earlier, Lillie and Joe had also celebrated their marriage in the family home (for their official wedding photograph, Lillie and Joe waited until Jessie and John got married, then donned their formal clothes again to pose all together).

During their first year of marriage, Jessie and John operated four men's clothing stores in Seattle, according to the information contained in the Polk Directory. One was at 1301 First Avenue, and two were next door to each other at 204 and 206 Main Street. They expanded their business by becoming the proprietors of the Hotel Main next door at 208 Main Street. The fourth store was at 210 Second Avenue South. Jessie served as bookkeeper for their businesses, a responsibility she kept for several years.

A researcher who compiled a family history for Fred Danz's wife, Bess, said that, at this time, John had five stores including one in Tacoma and one in Spokane, in addition to the Hotel Main. John reportedly went bankrupt, or very close to it, during an economic downturn in 1912. While he was able to pull himself out of the financial pit, he never forgot the experience. He also never forgot those who helped him with loans, lenient terms, and payment extensions. Nor did he ever forget those who put additional demands and pressure on him. The episode was undoubtedly a critical factor in John's penchant for secrecy in his business dealings. He went through a great struggle but was able to keep the two stores at 1301 First Avenue and 210 Second Avenue South.

There are several stories about how John got into the theater business. According to family tradition, John was asked to manage the High Class Theatre at 210 Second Avenue South between Main and Jackson, right next to the clothing store that had moved from that space to number 208. The theater was a nickelodeon, one of the small halls that offered patrons one-reel, silent motion pictures lasting about fifteen or twenty minutes for the admission price of five cents. The titles varied from mini dramas to comedies to "actualities," what we now call documentaries. Competitive exhibitors added their own

Location of two of John Danz's early stores at 204 and 206
Main Street (Washington State Archives).

Location of 208-210 Second Avenue S, John Danz Clothing Co.
and High Class Theatre (Washington State Archives)

organ or piano music to spice up the show. The musician supplied
the melody and tempo he thought appropriate to the scene being
displayed. The store at 208 Second Avenue South was John Danz
Clothing Company.[1]

Being the intelligent businessman that he was, John soon began
to use the theater to do cross-promotions with his store such as, "Buy
a suit and get free tickets to the theater," or "Bring in your theater
ticket stub and get a free pair of socks!" John does not seem to have
advertised in Seattle's three daily newspapers or the several weeklies.
He may have relied on handbills but probably counted on the location near Pioneer Square and the railroad and steamship terminals to
provide his customers. He soon found that all those people spending
their nickels turned a respectable profit at the theater.

Another version of the story claims that John got into the
theater business by setting out benches in a vacant building next to
his clothing store and showing movies for five cents. A third version
places this theater in a vacant lot, but that seems unlikely. An open air
venue might permit viewers to avoid paying their admission. Then, as
now, it often rained in Seattle, making an outdoor theater impractical.

The most likely version is this tale from Fred Danz, who worked
in the company from the age of eleven.

> My father started in the Nickelodeon business about 1914
> or 1915 down in an area that no longer exists in the city
> of Seattle, which was near Pioneer Square. [However,
> the High Class Theatre is listed in the city directory of
> 1912, which leads me to believe that John started the
> Nickelodeon earlier than Fred thought.] It doesn't exist
> because they straightened Second Avenue [in 1928] to
> help compensate for the fact that the original pioneers'
> two sections didn't match. They straightened Second
> Avenue so where it now goes south to join Fourth Avenue

---

1   In keeping with the custom of the time, if not grammatical convention, John and
other exhibitors named each of their houses "theatre." Theatre usually refers to the art form.
Theater refers to the building. I suspect that by the time someone pointed this out to John,
he was committed to calling his theaters theatres. This company tradition continued into
the twenty-first century.

South went right through the area where my father had his first businesses. He started a nickelodeon next to his haberdashery store on the theory that the nickelodeon would bring more customers past his haberdashery store. And soon, of course, he was making more money from the Nickelodeon than he was from the haberdashery. So he recognized which pair of socks he wanted to wear.

Late in life, Jessie related that John didn't expect much of the venture. He intended to run the theater for just a little while before expanding his haberdashery into that space. The building was not torn down and was still standing when the city took photos of all Seattle buildings in the 1930s; when the extension of Second Avenue South was put through, only the back half of the building was destroyed.

Before his marriage, John bought a house at 2406 Day Street. He never lived in the house and used the rental income as collateral for loans. He sold the house in 1914 and probably put the proceeds into the company. This sale may have made the purchase of the Crown Theatre possible in 1915. Of 1915, John later wrote:

> At that time I had two theatres, one of them called the High Class Theatre, a 250-seat house located in the skid row district of our city, charging an admission price of five cents. The other one, called the Crown Theatre, was located on First Avenue between Madison and Spring Streets. This was a slightly better location than the afore-mentioned theatre. The admission price was also five cents and the seating capacity was about the same as that of the High Class Theatre.

During 1915, director D. W. Griffiths released his full-length motion picture, *Birth of a Nation*. The great success of the film—despite its pro-Confederate racist theme—compelled production companies to shift to longer, more carefully scripted stories. The nickelodeon format phased out, but not short features and not the theater business. The advent of longer shows, perhaps, helped take the edge off

Washington's most recent social experiment. As of January 1, 1916, the sale and manufacture of intoxicating liquor throughout the state was banned. Saloons closed (officially), and Seattleites had to find something else to do with their afternoons and evenings.

In 1914, John operated six clothing stores. One, called Western Salvage Company, operated for only about a year at 707 Second Avenue. I found the first listing for Sterling Men's Wear at 608 First Avenue in 1915, the same year in which John formally incorporated the company. I don't know how he hit upon the name Sterling—an adjective for "excellent" or "valuable" taken from the title for British money. If later events are at all instructive, he stumbled across the name in the newspaper and liked it. He might also have seen the Sterling Building on First Avenue. Or maybe the word simply appealed to him because of its meaning.

The articles of incorporation include, as one of the purposes of the company:

> to buy, own, sell, mortgage and hypothecate [to pledge property as collateral without transfer of title] real and personal property of all kinds. To rent real and personal property of all kinds, and to subscribe for, own, sell and dispose of stock in other corporations ... The capital stock of the company shall be the sum of $10,000.00.

In the initial stock sale, J. J. Friedman purchased ninety-nine shares for $9,900, and D. P. Mikesell purchased one share for $100. The Articles of Incorporation for Sterling Men's Wear were filed on December 23 by directors J. J. Friedman and D. P. Mikesell. Sterling Men's Wear was originally incorporated for fifty years but later was incorporated in perpetuity. Long after he left haberdashery John continued to use this corporate vehicle to hold land leases and other entities for his growing theater company. Sterling Men's Wear was not dissolved until 1972. John appears to have developed the habit of remaining in the background on paper, seeking not to have his name associated with the business ventures he created. This could have been because he had a problem owning anything in his own name after the bankruptcy in 1912.

The directors elected John president of Sterling Men's Wear. On June 30, 1916, the City of Seattle issued a business license to Sterling Men's Wear with D. P. Mikesell and W. Karpes listed as trustees. In the subsequent share offering, original shares were exchanged for the new shares. Jessie's sister, Freda Mohr, held 230 shares in trust for Simon Danz. The books of Sterling Men's Wear indicate that there were nineteen people employed in the store when it opened. One of many things of interest to me was the salaries paid. For example, clerk J. Cohen earned $25 per week, probably for six days, working ten or twelve hours a day.

An agreement between J. Friedman and S. Danz of Astoria, Oregon, made on February 14, 1917, states that Friedman owns ninety-eight shares of the capital stock of Sterling Men's Wear Co. and that "John Dans [*sic*] owns and will be entitled to one share when he pays the balance of the purchase price thereof." John's brother, Simon, bought these original ninety-eight shares for $9,000.

According to Fred, Joe Friedman was a very successful insurance broker when he lived in Seattle. He and Lillie moved to Los Angeles in about 1921, where he first had a store where he repaired furniture. Later they moved to the San Fernando Valley where Joe had a chicken and egg farm in the 1940s. I was also told that Lillie ended up doing most of the work on the farm, which she didn't like, so she went out and got a job in the local post office, eventually serving as postmistress of Pacoima. Joe was never very successful in his business ventures in California, but when John asked him why he didn't return to Seattle and his successful insurance career, he replied that he would rather be broke in LA than a millionaire in Seattle.

Simon Danz married Allie Morris in 1912. He continued to work for Louis in the clothing stores until they moved to Astoria sometime in1914 or 1915.

John paid $750 up front for the shares of Sterling Men's Wear and was to pay $750 a month until the full purchase price was paid. All rights and privileges attached to the stock vested in Simon from the date of the agreement. John soon owned all the shares of Sterling Men's Wear, so, although I don't have proof, it seems apparent that he provided funds to Simon for his original purchase of the shares belonging to Friedman as well as those that Freda held for Simon.

David P. Mikesell became an important person in the early years of the company. He was a single, thirty-one-year-old native of Ohio who lived in a boarding house at 2809 Washington Street. Through his hard work, he earned John's trust. Although a director and stockholder, he appears in the books of Sterling Men's Wear as a clerk in September 1916. On his draft registration in 1918, Mikesell listed his occupation as a theatrical manager for Globe Amusement Company, and his work address was 117 Occidental Avenue, which was apparently the company offices.

John did not like others to know his business and worried that people would raise the price of their properties if they knew he was the buyer. To get around this, Mikesell often made deals in his own name and then turned the property over to John. After John created the Globe Amusement Company in 1917 (D. P. Mikesell was president, and Freda Mohr was secretary and treasurer), Mikesell purchased the lease on the Colonial Theatre Building uptown at 1514 Fourth Avenue at Pike Street and then sold the lease to Globe Amusement. John then incorporated the Acme Theatre Company by having David Mikesell and W. Karpes form the corporation with capital stock of 250 shares valued at $100 each. Karpes was president and owned ten shares. Mikesell was secretary with ten shares. W. Karpes was a jeweler who owned his own business. His wife, Elizabeth, was J. J. Friedman's sister. John kept most of his business within the family, with Freda Mohr, Simon Danz, and J. J. Friedman holding stock for him. This seems to be how he maintained control over his businesses without appearing to own them on paper.

John recognized the economy of scale in operating several theaters. Once he learned how to run one house and worked out the problems with it, he could easily acquire and operate a second, third, or fourth. As employees gained experience and proved their worth, he could move them between locations.

The main section of Seattle's business district was still centered around the Smith Tower (1914), but a strong retail core was already growing uptown near Third and Pine, where Westlake Avenue began back then. Fred reported:

> My father acquired two facilities in that area. He was aided in getting started by friends that were in allied businesses. None of them had any capital base or wealth, so they assisted each other with an informal sort of credit system among themselves.

Colonial Theatre, 1514 Fourth Avenue, ca. 1931.
(UW Special Collections, negative no. UW9110.)

They all had come to Seattle as young men, working hard to establish their businesses and secure their futures. While I couldn't find anyone who recalled the names of the men with whom John traded, I did learn that one was clothier Jacob Berkman, a close family friend throughout his life and the grandfather of my stepmother, Carolyn Blumenthal Taylor Danz. Berkman held a note from John for $405, dated December 29, 1914.

John knew that in the retail world the three critical factors were location, location, and location. But he soon discovered that things were a bit different in the theater business. "The key to the motion-picture industry then," Fred explained in 1986, "and to a great extent now is the ability to acquire the principal films."

Note from John Danz to J. Berkman & Bro.,
December 29, 1914.

Motion pictures were distributed on an exclusive basis within a market. Theater operators competed to win bookings of major productions and big names. The popularity of movies and movie stars exploded on the national and international scene. The theater that featured the first run of a Theda Bara, a Clara Bow, or a Mary Pickford film could guarantee a full house at top prices. And films had relatively short shelf lives. Once fans had seen a picture, they were unlikely to pay full price to see it again. New features were the key to success in the theater business. People still wanted to see second-run films, but the tickets were cheaper.

The theater business also caught the interest of other members of the family. In 1913, Louis, Simon, and Joseph bought the Imperial Theatre at 706 First Avenue, which they operated until 1918. Within a few years, they also built and operated the Rialto and Isis theaters. In April 1917, Louis sold his interest in these theaters to his son Joseph, but this may have been a premature decision. That same month the United States entered the Great War—World War I—and Seattle boomed again. Workers arrived to build ships for the fleet. Soldiers and sailors on furlough and liberty crowded city streets. The army established Camp Lewis near Tacoma, and the navy built a training camp on Portage Bay next to the University of Washington. Seattle businesses flourished during the brief but intense conflict.

In a classified ad in the *Seattle Daily Times* of May 5, 1918, John offered, "Show cases, wall cases, window fixtures, and shelving must be sold" at 608 First Avenue. This would appear to be the end of John's career in clothing. The books for Sterling Men's Wear stop at the end of June 1918.

The theater business was doing well enough that on October 20, 1918 John and Jessie bought two pianos: a grand piano for $500 and an upright for $125. I don't know what they did with the second piano during these years, but in later years the grand piano sat in the living room of their wonderful apartment on Queen Anne Hill. I remember an upright (albeit a much newer model) in the apartment of a neighbor who used it to practice so she could accompany John on his mandolin. When John died in 1961 the upright piano came to me and sits in my recreation room to this day.

With the violence and bloodshed of war came pestilence. The massive movements of populations during the First World War contributed to the rapid spread of an influenza pandemic. On October 3, 1918, influenza officially hit Seattle. The disease apparently arrived in Seattle aboard a trainload of U.S. Navy recruits from Philadelphia. Over seven hundred trainees came down with the illness, and three died in University of Washington dormitories, converted into hospitals. Victims experienced the rapid onset of high fever, which produced pulmonary edema and death. The appearance of the disease on the East Coast a month before allowed Seattle to plan. Authorities began by banning dances and spitting, then all public gatherings, including those in theaters. Streetcar windows were ordered left open. At the end of October, six-ply gauze masks became required in public. Funerals of victims were limited to six persons. Nurses tending to influenza patients found themselves evicted by terrified landlords. Some residents fled the city.

The ban on public gatherings officially ended in January 1919, but another calamity cut into revenues for businesses and theater owners. On February 6, 1919, labor leaders called a general strike in

Seattle in sympathy with shipyard workers protesting the loss of jobs after the Armistice. It was the first general strike in the nation's history, and many feared a spread of the revolution that tore apart Russia. For five days, the city was paralyzed as workers stayed home. Businesses, including movie theaters, remained shuttered. It wouldn't be the last time that the interests of organized labor and John Danz clashed.

In 1919, the Doughboys came marching home to look for work. The nation experienced a general economic slump as war industries closed and farm prices fell. Employers found they could pressure workers to tear up union cards and accept lower wages for jobs of any kind.

On January 31, 1919, Globe Amusement Company was incorporated although it appears to have been already operating for at least a year. The company was capitalized at $10,000 with David Mikesell owning $100 worth of stock and Freda Mohr holding $9,900. Once again, it seems apparent from this historic distance that John funded the purchase of the stock held by Freda. The corporate seal for Globe was a circle within a circle. In 1919, John also added two theaters to his growing organization: the Star on Occidental Avenue South, just south of Yesler Way, built around 1897 as a dance hall, and the Capitol, up at 1508 Third Avenue between Pine and Pike. John co-owned the Capitol with Northwest Newsreel through Globe Amusement and reopened it as Seattle Telenews, showing newsreels all day.

Seattle Telenews.

Globe Amusement purchased a Wurlitzer organ the same year for $7,000, more than the price of a good home. On December 31, we find the first mention of the Circuit Theatre Company, another entity set up to own a theater.

During these years John and Jessie's family grew. On September 20, 1913, they welcomed their first child, daughter Dorothy, into their new home at B305 29th Avenue South. Son William (Bill) was born on January 22, 1915, and their third child, Frederic (Fred), arrived on February 28, 1918. John and Jessie moved four times in their first six years of marriage until they rented a home on present-day 22nd Avenue, where they lived from 1920 until 1934. Bill remembered living in this house when he went off to school.

John Danz family residence 922 22nd Avenue North (later 22nd Avenue) 1920 to 1934. (Washington State Archives.)

(Bill's best friend, Melvin Weinstein lived on 23rd, the next block over, and they walked to school together every day. Mel was Bill's best friend all the way through Garfield High School. They kept in touch throughout their lives until Mel died in his eighties. Mel had moved to Los Angeles in his sixties, and when Bill and his wife, Carolyn, spent the winters in LA, Bill and Mel would have lunch, play cards, and enjoy their continuing friendship.)

The Danzes had three young children at home, and Jessie remembered that while she continued to do the bookkeeping for the theaters, she was able to do the work at home and take care of the children at the same time. She proudly said the children never had a meal without her being there. On those occasions when she had to go to in to the office to work, Fred recalled that Jessie would drop him off with the organist at the theater who kept an eye on him during the performance.

Big changes occurred within the company during 1920. John and Jessie had secured ownership of all the capital stock of both Sterling Men's Wear and of Globe Amusement Company and became trustees. Friedman and Mikesell dropped off the list of officers of Sterling Men's Wear, and Freda Mohr and Frank Edwards (mayor of Seattle from 1928 to 1931) were added to the board, Edwards as president, Jessie as secretary, with John as a trustee but not an officer. Jessie soon resigned as secretary, and Freda took on the role with a salary of $50 a week.

John received a salary from Acme Theatre Company of $150 a week, and Jessie received a salary of $50. From Globe Theatre Company, John received $250 a week and Jessie another $50. Five hundred dollars then would be more than $5,000 today. The Danzes took home the equivalent of more than $24,000 a month. At the end of 1920, Globe Amusement declared a dividend of $15,000.

John now operated five theaters—the High Class, the Crown, the Colonial, the Star, and Seattle Telenews. He had divested himself of the men's clothing business that had brought him to Seattle.

THE MOVIES TALK

❧ 1921–1930 ❧

As in the rest of the country, the 1920s were good to Seattle, certainly to Seattle business. A recession followed the First World War, but the city bounced back with a vengeance, particularly downtown. Developers and elected officials embarked on a construction program the likes of which would not be seen again until the 1980s. The Olympic Hotel (1924), four more floors for Frederick and Nelson, the Bon Marché (1928), the King County Courthouse (1929), the Northern Life Tower (1929), Harborview Hospital (1931), Sand Point Naval Air Station (1925), and Boeing Field (1928) are just a few of the projects. West Coast Air Transport launched coast-to-coast air service—fifty-six hours to New York. Seattle's first female mayor, Bertha Knight Landes, took office in 1926. The Smith Tower remained the tallest building west of the Mississippi.

Seattle also built outside the city limits. Dams at the Gorge and Diablo on the Skagit River and a powerhouse at Newhalem supplied enough electricity so that every Seattle neighborhood had current. Seattle increased its use of electricity by almost five-fold. Police and Prohibition agents pursued moonshiners in a perpetual cat-and-mouse game. One former policeman, Roy Olmstead, became a full-time bootlegger and something of a local folk hero with his own radio show. Despite Prohibition, it wasn't too hard for serious drinkers to slake their thirsts in speakeasies. The popularity and influence of movies continued to grow.

At the end of 1920, John took an unusually large lump sum of $13,000 as salary from Acme, plus another $1300 salary for Jessie. I hesitate to make any assumption as to why this large sum was taken at a time when the average income for individuals was less than $500 a year, but given the growth of the company, it seems evident that John used his own money to capitalize the business rather than issue stock.

In October 1920, the deed to Globe Amusement transferred to Jessie and John. Between the end of 1921, and early in 1923, they placed four different mortgages on the Capitol Theatre. Two of these were funded by individual investors and two by banks. By the end of 1924, they had satisfied the mortgages to both Marine National Bank and to Seaboard Securities. John used debt to move his businesses forward but did not usually embrace long-term obligations.

John continued to learn the theater business. He worked eighteen hours a day operating his five theaters and, according to Jessie, thought nothing of it. He almost always came home for dinner, and when the children had gone to bed, he left to visit theaters. He continued this routine for most of his life, and when his sons, Bill and Fred, began working for the company full time in the late 1930s, he expected them to do the same.

John was a demanding boss, and his standards were always at the highest level; he expected everyone in his company to have the same work ethic. Given the movie houses further uptown with their elaborate architecture and ostentatious wall hangings and murals—the Coliseum (1916), the Blue Mouse (1920), the Orpheum (1927), the Paramount (1928), and the Fox (1928)—John needed to compete in some way. Any venue that hosted hundreds of visitors every day, many munching popcorn in the dark, could easily become worn and soiled. John saw to it that every patron was provided with a clean, high-quality motion picture or vaudeville experience. On his nightly visits, he noticed everything from a burned-out light, a restroom needing attention, or an unswept walkway. Any deficiency he found unacceptable. This ideal never changed, even when John employed district managers to inspect the theaters. John instilled in his staff and the entire organization a high sense of excellence when other capitalists were satisfied with "good enough." To be sure, John felt a great deal of competition from the likes of Alexander Pantages and John Hamrick and their opulent movie houses, but John met quantity with quality and with value.

One of the ways John learned to compete with these other theaters was through his mastery of showmanship. He soon became well known as a master of promotion, which he called exploitation. Theater managers, coordinating with the company office, created elaborate special advertising, both in and outside of the theater, to attract viewers. They dressed staff in elaborate costumes, hired people to perform outside of the theater, and created unique banners and placards for each show.

Theater staff ready for the public to arrive to enjoy the new 1920 silent film, *The Virgin of Stamboul*, starring Priscilla Dean and directed by Tod Browning.

Just as the 1920s roared for Seattle, it "boomed" for John and Jessie, more than just figuratively.

Seattle had had a strong organized labor movement since the turn of the century. Almost every group of workers from milliners to waitresses to warehousemen formed bargaining units. The unions were so popular in Seattle that the militant and notorious Industrial Workers of the World—the Wobblies—found little traction for their cries for one big union.

Employers naturally resisted demands for higher wages, shorter hours, and better working conditions. The eight-hour day and the forty-hour week remained a dream for most workers. One major bone of contention was the "closed shop," an agreement that all employees must belong to a union. With all employees of a business and even an entire sector organized, unions held great leverage in bargaining. In those days, there were no laws regulating representation or requiring employers to recognize unions. The closed shop was countered by the employers' "open shop" or "right to work" position. Open shop proponents asserted that a worker had a right not to join a union if he chose.

The Bolshevik Revolution in Russia in 1917 and the General Strike in 1919 unleashed a governmental backlash against socialists, communists, anarchists, and labor unions in an era called the Red Scare. U.S. Attorney General Mitchell Palmer ordered the arrests of thousands deemed seditious. Seattle police staged "Palmer Raids" and rounded up hundreds they considered to be "reds." Suspects were booked into jail on the charge of "hold for Attorney General."

The theater business saw its share of union troubles. Beginning in 1921, John found himself in the middle of one of the longest and most intractable labor disputes in the history of Seattle. He fought the amusement industry labor unions for fourteen years.

Historian Jonathan Dembo gives us in "John Danz and the Seattle Amusement Trades Strike, 1921-1935," *Pacific Northwest Quarterly*, Vol. 71:4 (Autumn 1980), an in-depth picture of the antagonists and the circumstances surrounding the labor disputes. There were four main unions and several smaller ones that made up what was called the Theatrical Federation. The largest of these was the Seattle Association of Musicians, Local 76 of the American Federation of Musicians, followed by the Local 154 of the Motion Picture Operators Union. Local 15 of Theatrical and Stage Employees Union and Local

6 of the Building Services Employees Union joined the musicians in demands for recognition and contracts.

Theodore Henry "Dad" Wagner was the longtime president of Musicians Local 76, and William J. Douglas, the business manager of the Seattle Symphony was another prominent union leader.

At the Seattle Telenews, John had a single electric organ to accompany the silent newsreels. He employed two organists who split the week between them. He had installed a Wurlitzer at the Colonial in 1918 and likely had two organists there as well, also splitting the week (although the feature film houses probably had shorter hours than Telenews, which ran all day and into the evening). The union told John that this practice was hurting his business. They suggested trying out a six-man orchestra for a couple of months. John agreed that if their point was proved he would sign a contract. The test proved highly profitable for both John and the musicians. In March 1920, John recognized the union and began to employ the very best artists he could find. John's brother, Joe, also recognized the union for his three theaters.

The 1921 recession cut deeply into attendance and John had to make massive pay and personnel cuts. He refused to make exceptions for his union employees, locking out those who would not accept his terms. When the union protested, he went so far as to show the leaders the dismal, near-bankruptcy figures on his books. The union men refused to concede and continued to try to get John to negotiate.

By the time the employers association, the Allied Amusement Interests of Washington, began negotiations for the 1922 contract, John was committed to an open shop alliance. The employers asked for a 40 percent wage cut and reductions in personnel at downtown theaters. They also offered to expand working hours in order to maintain income levels for their employees.

The unions reacted by striking against Joe Danz's theaters. The other theater owners responded by locking out their union members and replacing them with non-union employees. Positions continued to harden until John was placed on the "unfair" list by the musicians local.

Things continued to escalate with boycotts of theaters and stink bombs detonated in auditoriums all over town to disrupt the shows. Union leaders claimed that John bombed his own theaters in order to get public opinion on his side. Finally, on December 27, 1922, a dynamite blast destroyed the family car in front of the Danz home. If John had been resistant to the unions, this reckless act that threatened his wife and children must only have solidified his position.

Picketing, threats, intimidation, and lawsuits continued for years. The unions made great strides with other theater owners over the next few years until John was the last man standing. He was the only owner still resisting the unions' efforts when, on February 26, 1925, the State Supreme Court granted John's request for a permanent injunction against the picketing. The Court held that the concept of peaceful picketing was meaningless and that the purpose of picketing was coercive.

This didn't end the battle. The unions appealed. In 1930, the ruling was overturned. But by this time, the unions' position had eroded with the advent of talkies. The need for musicians and stagehands plummeted. In the end, the musicians decided to direct their efforts away from the Sterling theater chain and concentrate on the more lucrative nightclub and radio employers. Negotiations with John continued into December 1934 with little to show for it. The unions filed a complaint to the National Recovery Administration's regional labor board over the 1929 dismissal of employees for their union membership. The unions prevailed, and after an audit of the Sterling books, the labor board ruled that John owed the fired employees $20,000 in back wages.

John resisted a settlement but was eventually forced back to the bargaining table. On April 2, 1935, he signed a contract with the Musicians Union, establishing wages and hours. The agreement also ended any pending litigation against him.

The union victory proved pyrrhic. By the time the contract went into effect, John employed musicians in just one of his theaters. All the rest had been converted to sound motion pictures. Both sides learned a hard lesson regarding the cost of such disputes. For the next fifty years or more, peace reigned between the Theatrical Federation and the Sterling companies.

John's eldest son, Bill, began working in the theaters in about 1926 when he was eleven years old. He started as a doorman in the State Theatre, located at First and Madison, which had two entrances—one on First Avenue and the other up the hill a little way on Madison—and two cashiers. Bill recalled that when a customer came in either entrance the doorman took his ticket, tore it in two, and returned one half to the customer. While Bill thought that it was pretty boring most of the time, just standing around waiting for people to enter, he did appreciate the showgirls in the stage show. He thought they were the prettiest creatures on earth, and he enjoyed the songs they sang.

Despite the picketing and other nuisances, movies continued to captivate the fans who lined up for tickets. Stars like Mary Pickford, Douglas Fairbanks, and Rudolph Valentino achieved unheard of celebrity in popular culture. In March 1927, John Hamrick's Blue Mouse demonstrated Vitaphone, a phonograph record synchronized with the film *Don Juan* with musical score and sound effects but no dialogue. "Talkies" continued to evolve, and at the end of 1927, the Blue Mouse (an addition to the Sterling chain in 1964) tried out Phonofilm sound-on-film technology in a newsreel of Charles Lindbergh's flight across the Atlantic. *The Jazz Singer* with Al Jolson premiered later that month as the first feature film with sound using Vitaphone. One limitation of Vitaphone was that the record could easily fail to synchronize with the film. These efforts fell by the technological wayside when sound-on-film proved to be of better quality and easier to handle (no disks distributed with the films).

The Blue Mouse had been built as a silent movie theater in the early 1920s and became the first Seattle theater to convert to sound. Converting from silent to sound movies was neither cheap nor easy. Soundproofing, new screens, and the sound equipment all added to the expense with upgrades running upwards of $6,000 each. To pay for these changes, theaters found it necessary to increase their ticket prices. Instead of ten cents for children and twenty-five cents for adults, children's tickets might go to fifteen cents and adults to thirty-five.

Tickets to *The Jazz Singer* were fifty cents. The typical show consisted of an Our Gang movie and another short film or two followed by the full-length main feature. Some of John's theaters still presented Vaudeville acts, but people were going to the movies in droves.

In 1927, John took on the management of the Palace Hippodrome—"The Hip"—and the Cheerio (later named the Queen Anne) and Winter Garden theaters. At the end of the decade, he owned eight theaters and had an office staff of six. During 1928, the businesses did well; Globe Amusement Company declared a dividend of $15,000.

Palace Hippodrome.
(Post-Intelligencer Collection, Museum of History & Industry.)

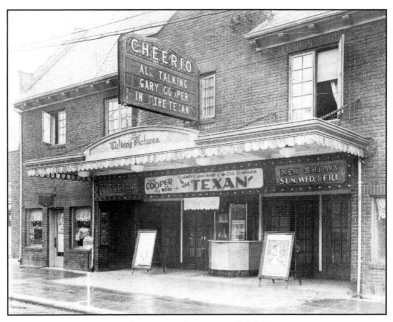

Cheerio Theatre, 1930.

Winter Garden Theatre, 1928.

Although John worked long and hard, he always made time for the family. Bill remembers playing football and other games with his father and brother in the yard of the family home. There were frequent outings during the summer for picnics and swimming at Seward Park, often joined by their extended family of grandparents, aunts, uncles, and cousins. Bill and Dorothy became quite strong swimmers, and during the summer of 1927 when Bill was twelve and Dorothy almost fourteen, the two of them swam across Lake Washington, accompanied by their father and other relatives in a row boat. Holidays were also celebrated with the extended family, although the children thought the long Passover Sedars boring.

Hannah and Louis Danz and Anna and Maurice Mohr, 1920.

Extended family at the beach, Lake Washington, 1921. Back row from left: Jessie Danz, John Danz, Freda Mohr, Abraham Suransky, Jennie Mohr, Si Danz. Front row from left: Fred Danz, Lucille Weslow, Bill Danz, Dorothy Danz, Freda Carrol, Ted Carrol, Sarah Carrol, George Carrol.

Jessie became involved in the life of the community very early in her married life. She served on the board of Jewish Family Service (originally called the Hebrew Benevolent Society) for more than thirty years and served as president for thirteen of those years, starting in 1929. She served on the Board of the Federated Jewish Fund (now known as Jewish Federation) and also sat on the board of Washington Children's Home for many years. After Dorothy got married in 1934, she joined her mother as a member of the Jewish Family Service board.

Hard Times to Victory

❧ 1930–1945 ❧

The Great Depression of the 1930s found its origins in many places. The popular perception is that the economic bubble of the Roaring Twenties burst with the Wall Street Crash in 1929. The Dow Jones industrial average lost 40 percent of its value in eight weeks. Credit dried up, wealth evaporated, businesses closed, and the unemployed and homeless queued up for relief. There were other factors in the downturn as well. A new set of protective tariffs cut into trade and markets overseas. A persistent drought and falling farm prices devastated agriculture, once the backbone of the national economy.

The hard times didn't really hit Seattle until the late summer of 1930 as traffic across the waterfront dwindled and longshoremen, seamen, teamsters, and their employers found themselves on the beach. Businesses even remotely connected to trade suffered as well. Limited credit meant that construction stopped almost entirely. When the need for lumber dropped, work in mills and forests went away too. Not just the unemployed, but the underemployed—those working but bringing home far less than before—suffered along with the rest of the country. City employees had their work and paychecks slashed by a quarter. When policemen and firemen did get paid, it was often with warrants—IOUs—which employees then tried to sell at a discount for cash. The library system fired every married librarian, reasoning that her husband should care for her. It was a depression not just economically but psychologically as well.

The Depression still offered some opportunities, and the 1930s saw a significant growth in the theater business for John and his companies. With funds borrowed from friends and banks, he pooled his assets to make deals.

When the Depression broke over Seattle, John owned and/or operated the Star, the Capitol, the Portola, the Colonial, the Palace Hippodrome, the Seattle Telenews theaters. Then, in June 1930, just as the downturn began, John formed the Far West Theatre Corporation "to establish, maintain, operate, manage, and control a theatre or theatres, a place or places of amusement etc." Within months, he took on the operation of the Granada Theatre in West Seattle at 5011 California Avenue Southwest and the Roycroft Theatre at 19th and Roy Street through his Far West Theatre Company. John became a partner in the Granada Theatre Company, and in March of 1934, he became the president. Eventually he became the sole owner. On occasion, John elected to retain personal rather than company ownership, but I don't know what his strategy was.

Granada Theatre, 5011 California Avenue Southwest, 1932.
(UW Special Collections, negative no. UW14633.)

Roycroft Theatre, 19th Avenue and Roy Street, 1932.
(UW Special Collections, negative no. UW14662.)

He also purchased the Florence Theatre at 512 Second Avenue for $15,000.

The Roosevelt Theatre building and property at 515 Pike Street joined his theater chain in the early 1930s. The same year John used two less well-known men to purchase the Portola in West Seattle, which was transferred to him a few years later. The Portola underwent a major remodel during 1941, reopening in January 1942 as the Admiral Theatre. In 1930, the Cheerio at 1529 Queen Anne Avenue North became the Queen Anne Theatre.

The most enduring images of the Depression in Seattle were the homeless encampments dubbed "Hoovervilles" after President Herbert Hoover, who did not feel government had any responsibility to resolve problems with the economy. There were several Hoovervilles throughout Seattle, but the one at the foot of South Atlantic Street on the waterfront was the largest and most photographed. Hundreds

Portola Theatre, 2343 California Avenue SW, 1930
(UW Special Collections).

Queen Anne Theatre, 1529 Queen Anne Avenue N, 1932
(UW Special Collections)

of unemployed men and a few women tacked together shacks out of scrap wood and cardboard. They even formed a communal government to regulate health and behavior. Unemployment in Seattle was at 11 percent in April 1930 and rose to 25.4 percent in January 1935. More than half the unemployed were forty years of age or older.

Despite being able to make some important acquisitions, John spoke later of how he had to pick and choose between bills—which ones to pay in full, which ones could wait—in order to keep his businesses moving forward. Items like salaries and film usage fees got paid promptly. Even a one-day delay in delivery of a hit movie meant that patrons might spend the twenty-five cents, set aside for one show a week, at another theater. Without films, he was out of business. And he had to meet every payroll.

The light and water bills waited longer. The utility companies had so many accounts in arrears that they were grateful for a reliable, if slow-paying, commercial customer. When he got a few months behind paying the power company, he was able to secure an agreement that he could be three months late in paying his bill. Each month he took care of the oldest bill.

He made a similar agreement with Leslie Stusser of Stusser Electric, supplier of the bulbs for the projectors. The Stussers were social friends as well as business associates. They agreed that John could be three months behind. At the end of the three months, John would give Stusser a note that could be taken to the bank and cashed. John didn't have to pay off the note to the bank for another three months, essentially giving him a six-month break.

He also worked with the same consortium of friends who had supported one another early in their careers. When a payroll needed to be paid, John might have to borrow the day's receipts from a friend at another theater or from a colleague not related to entertainment. Later, he would turn his day's receipts over to that friend or to another colleague, enabling him to pay his bills or meet his payroll. These businessmen carefully staggered payments and payroll periods to keep each other afloat. This became, in effect, an underground banking system, relying almost wholly on trust.

Bill recalled just one time when it was obvious that John was extremely worried and angry about business. A competitor wanted to buy him out and had formed a group of investors to join him. When they offered to buy his business out from under him, John naturally refused, but the action by this combination of adversaries disturbed him deeply. He never forgot the people that helped him or those who did not, and it reinforced his need for secrecy.

In December 1948, banker and businessman Joshua Green wrote to John on the occasion of the opening of the Magnolia Theatre, "You have made some fine footprints here, young man, and made them on some pretty hard and uphill roads!"

John wrote back thanking Green for his thoughtful message, but included a paragraph reminding him that, "The most serious trouble I encountered was when your bank and one of its clients conspired against me during the worst part of the great depression."

The company owned a parcel of land across the street from the Paramount Theatre at Ninth Avenue and Pine Street on which a gas station was located. Fifteen-year-old Bill Danz worked as the manager of the gas station during the summer of 1933, and Fred told me that he also worked there when he was fifteen or sixteen but that John was never able to make the station profitable so he closed it down and eventually sold the land.

John's brother and sister-in-law, Simon and Allie, had moved to Astoria in 1914, where they also took up the theater business. Bill Danz remembers visiting them at the movie house they operated out on a pier. He told me that Si either could not, or simply did not get, fire insurance, and eventually the theater burned down. Si moved back to Seattle and approached John to help him to get started in the theater business again. John called his bookkeeper in and said something to the effect of, "Tell Si how much we're overdrawn." The bookkeeper related the dismal circumstances: John was fighting very hard just to keep his business together. Joseph Danz also sought help from his brother but came away disappointed. Bill believed that surviving the Depression without losing his business was his father's major achievement. But John's inability to help his brothers drove a wedge between them, especially between John and Joseph.

The hard times led to a resurgence of organized labor and progressive politics. John's old colleague, Mayor Frank Edwards, found himself recalled by voters after he fired J. D. Ross, the popular head of Seattle City Light. At the root of the firing was Edwards's reactionary response to radicals' attempts to organize the unemployed and his opposition to public ownership of electrical utilities. As unemployment skyrocketed, thousands turned out for demonstrations and marches demanding reform and even revolution. Although John did not engage in politics, we can assume that groups like the Unemployed Citizens' League and the Washington Commonwealth Federation met with his disapproval.

The year 1935 brought John's formation of the Third & University Corporation, which purchased the Pantages Theatre together with the Pantages Theatre Building (1915) on the northeast corner of Third and University. The Pantages had been built by Alexander Pantages (1876–1936), the unlettered Greek immigrant who assembled a theater and vaudeville empire up and down the West Coast. At one point, he controlled seventy vaudeville theaters. He constructed large, elaborately decorated theater buildings seating as many as twenty-eight hundred people. The landmark structures featured stained glass, domed ceilings, gilt, bronze, and murals. The Seattle Pantages Theater was remodeled in 1925 but passed out of the Pantages empire in 1929.

When the purchase of the Pantages closed, John arrived home, saying he had to come up with a new name for the theater that began with a *P* because Alexander Pantages had installed giant *P*s all over the building. The observatory at Mount Palomar in California had recently appeared in the news, and this inspired John. The Palomar got a new marquee, and the building became the headquarters for Sterling Theatres. This wonderful theater was designed by Benjamin Marcus Priteca (1889–1971), who designed more than 125 theatres across North America. His works in Seattle included the major remodel of the Admiral Theatre in West Seattle in 1942 and the creation of the Magnolia Theatre in 1948. Priteca continued to provide architectural services for Sterling for many years and remained active as an architect well into his eighties. He died in Seattle in October 1971.

Rumor had it that the Palomar was haunted. Legend was that the corner was the site of a pioneer cemetery and when the graves were moved one grave was left behind. The ghost caused commotions felt during shows. The reality was less interesting: Great Northern Railway trains ran through a tunnel under Fourth Avenue causing the building to shake.

Palomar Theatre and Building, Third Avenue and University Street, 1938. (UW Special Collections Order No. SEA0446.) Insert: Palomar renamed New Rex Theatre, featuring stage shows in addition to feature films, 1935.

Long-time Seattle restaurateur John Franco (Franco's Hidden Harbor) told historian Paul Dorpat that during the 1930s one of John's tenants on an upper floor of the Palomar was a betting parlor (Sterling executive Zollie Volchok recalls that in the 1940s the neighborhood betting parlor was across the street above Green's Cigar Store).

The company continued to expand, purchasing the Uptown Theatre at the foot of Queen Anne Hill in 1936.

According to Fred, the Depression shook up the motion picture industry tremendously, albeit not in a destructive way. The drop in theater attendance forced the motion picture industry to reduce costs and cut prices for admission to ten or fifteen cents per ticket. This allowed patrons to see shows on a weekly basis without going broke. It also kept John in business and his employees at work. The escape offered during two hours of music or drama or comedy helped keep and even form a national character.

Between 1936 and 1938, the books of Sterling Theatres show a mixed bag: the Roosevelt, Palomar, and Star theaters all consistently lost money during those years while the State and Colonial were up and down. The Capitol and Florence did well, sometimes quite well. The Florence Theatre, next door to the Smith Tower, made between one hundred and $300 in profits per week. The Star closed in 1938, perhaps because it was outmoded as a theater and was consistently going downhill.

Palomar Theatre staff in uniform, 1930s.

Motion pictures masked and mirrored the turmoil of the times. Opposite the visually stunning—even in black and white—productions of Busby Berkeley, delightful musicals with Shirley Temple, and the historical epics like *Mutiny on the Bounty* or mindless slapstick with W. C. Fields and the Marx Brothers were inspirational works like *Mr. Deeds Goes to Town* and *Lost Horizon*. Hollywood producer Jack Warner introduced viewers to the rising threat of Fascism while his contemporaries shied away from any controversy. The newsreels brought in the news of the world, from the rise of the Nazis in Germany and Jessie Owens's spectacular win at the 1936 Olympics to the kindly visage and comforting voice of President Franklin D. Roosevelt. There was something for everyone at the movies.

John's theaters were not part of the chains controlled by the Hollywood studios that got the first-run hits. He was able to book the hits in second run and B movies, which he showed at good prices in clean and well-maintained houses. His nightly attention to detail ensured a reputation for quality.

The final acquisition of the decade was the purchase of the lease for the Circle Theatre at the end of 1939. As before, John conducted this transaction using a man named Frank Jenkins acting on his behalf. The lease was purchased from S. Mukai for five years for $7500 at a monthly rent of $250.

On the domestic front, John's eldest child, Dorothy, married William (Bill) Forman on June 3, 1934. Bill was from The Dalles, Oregon, where his family was in the hide and fur business with a small general store. He came to Seattle to attend the University of Washington, where he met Dorothy, but because of the depression, he was forced to leave school and go home to The Dalles. He returned to Seattle to marry Dorothy when she graduated, and he joined Sterling shortly after their wedding. Their daughter, JoAnne, told me her dad was a bit of a country bumpkin when they were first married, but he was also brilliant and developed into a sophisticated, powerful, urbane, and highly respected businessman.

Bill Danz graduated from the University of Washington in 1936 with a degree in accounting at the age of twenty-one. He then followed his girlfriend, Selma Goldstein, to Oakland, where she attended Mills College. He found an accounting position in San Francisco so he could be close to her. She found the attention annoying. She had been looking forward to being on her own as a beautiful, young college coed in the Bay Area. Boy did that cramp her style! Her college career at Mills lasted only one year.

When she returned to Seattle and the University of Washington, Bill followed along and joined the Sterling Theatre Company. Bill and Selma were married on May 18, 1937. She was just turning nineteen, and he was twenty-two. They had three children: Barbara Jean born in June of 1938, Carolyn Ida ("Carolee") born in December of 1940, and Penelope Ruth ("Penny"), born in October of 1942.

Jessie and John had never owned their own home. In 1938, they partnered with their friend Sam Rubenstein to purchase the Narada Apartments at 25 West Highland Drive along the Counterbalance on the south slope of Queen Anne Hill. Their apartment on the top (fifth) floor was a wonderfully large apartment with a magnificent view of Puget Sound, downtown Seattle, Mount Rainier, and Elliott Bay. Fred continued to live with his parents until he married in 1940.

Narada Apartments, 25 West Highland Drive.

Fred attended the University of Washington for a year or so, then left college around 1940 to join the company. He told me that he originally agreed to join the Zeta Beta Tau fraternity but found the pledge system silly and demeaning, so he quickly dropped out. He also felt he could learn more from his father than from his professors so he left the university too. He had attended the university just long enough to meet Selma Gold of Phoenix, Arizona. She had chosen the UW in order to work with Glenn Hughes, the very well-known and respected professor of drama. Fred and Selma courted until she graduated then married on March 15, 1940. Selma continued to pursue her theatrical interests but always seemed to regret that she hadn't had the opportunity to become a professional actress. She also suffered greatly from a leg ailment that was significantly aggravated by the cool damp Seattle climate. Selma and Fred had two children during their first four years of marriage: A son, T. Adam (Tad), was born in July of 1942, and daughter Laurie Gay arrived in September of 1944.

With two Selmas in the family, my sisters and I called Fred's wife "Selma Fred" and Fred's children called Bill's wife "Selma Jane."

Fred, on the other hand, was very content to learn and participate in the operation of the family company. He continued to be involved for the next sixty-nine years, until his death in 2009.

❦ ❦

The end of the Great Depression in the U.S. is marked with the defeat of France by Germany in June 1940. Hitler seemed insatiable in his territorial ambitions as Europe fell under German rule. Britain stood alone against Nazi aggression. Despite strong isolationist sentiments throughout the U.S., Congress enacted huge defense programs and a peacetime draft. Money flowed into Seattle to pay for new bombers and ships. Housing construction resumed, and the steam whistles in mills and logging camps sang again. The waterfront bustled anew. People brought home full-pay envelopes, and the birth rate climbed. With money in their pockets, consumers began to spend again. John Danz came through the lean years by carefully managing his daily cash flow and expanding his theater holdings. From the ostentatious

Palomar downtown to simpler neighborhood movie houses in West
Seattle and on Queen Anne and Capitol Hill, he sold tens of thousands of movie tickets a week. With both his sons in the business,
they enjoyed a greater reach than when John alone visited his five
theaters every night. In one letter, he reported that "the boys" had split
up the week, taking turns at these nightly visits. John continued his
nightly visits, often after the boys had completed their inspections.
They never knew when or where he would show up.

❧ ❧

Although cataclysmic and horrific for the rest of the world, the decade
of the 1940s and World War II were good for the business community in Seattle. When the U.S. entered the war in December 1941,
the Boeing plant and the shipyards were already running at capacity.
Tens of thousands of new residents arrived by train and auto to take
the new jobs and crowd into available housing. Seattle ranked as one
of the top three locations for war contracts per capita. Servicemen
stationed at McCord Field, Fort Lewis, Sand Point Naval Air Station,
Paine Field, Fort Lawton, the Puget Sound Naval Shipyard, and a
dozen other military installations in the region came to Seattle for
relaxation and entertainment. That included the movies.

In 1940, John began an expansion of the company through a
partnership with the financially distressed owners of the Columbia
Theatre Company, which owned theaters in the Longview and Kelso
area. By 1944, he bought the other partners out, and Sterling enjoyed
a significant presence in the Longview/Kelso region. During the same
period John bought the Roosevelt Theatre building at Fifth and Pike
as his personal property from Esana Company, one of the several
Sterling corporations. All the real property, furniture, and fixtures
were deeded to him in exchange for a mortgage of $72,000.

In April 1940, John's son-in-law Bill Forman resigned from
Sterling Theatres. After more than five years, he found it frustrating
and impossible to continue to work for John, a difficult taskmaster,
unwilling to accept the suggestions of others. John's style was not
unlike other self-made men who extend trust sparingly and keep

their own counsel. Bill also had bigger dreams for himself. After Bill Forman left, Fred Danz became secretary of all the Danz family corporate entities with Bill Danz serving as treasurer. Bill Forman and John Danz remained estranged for a few years. When Dorothy and her children attended family dinners at Jessie and John's apartment, Bill refused to attend. The arrangement was very hard on Dorothy, but she remained close to her parents. Before the war ended, however, John and Bill Forman were doing business together again. (Bill Forman went on to open drive-in theaters in the Seattle area, then moved his family to California where he developed Pacific Theatres and United Drive-in Theatres into the largest and one of the most successful theater companies in the country.)

Under the wartime economy, the government rationed strategic materials like rubber and gasoline. Anything that could go to the war effort was controlled. Gasoline went only to those who could demonstrate a need to travel by car. People could not get new telephone service because copper was critical to field radios and other electronic devices. Food and clothing were subjected to rationing systems. While construction of new military bases exploded along with housing for war workers, authorities imposed a ban on building places of civilian amusement. Consequently, John built no new theaters. But that didn't mean John couldn't plan for the time when the war would be over and building could resume.

In 1942, both the Third & University Corporation and Globe Amusement declared dividends. Sterling's Far West Theatre Company leased the Admiral Theatre from John and Jessie and purchased all the furniture and fixtures.

In 1943, John started a practice that continued for the life of the theater companies. He began making inter-company agreements to lease land, provide services, and supply equipment. In the earliest agreement I found, Sterling Theatres contracted with the Portola Company, another Danz entity, to supply all the equipment used for the Palomar Theatre. The Portola Company also held exclusive rights to provide the concessions. Similar arrangements were made among various Sterling entities. Land and buildings were often owned by one

company and leased to Sterling Theatres to operate. These manipula-
tions limited the tax liability of the various companies during a time
when the corporate tax rate grew astronomically. In July, the Portola
Company was merged into Progressive Company, one of the businesses wholly owned by Jessie and John.

The Granada Theatre Company had the highest earnings in its
history in 1943. It declared a dividend of $7.50 per share, up from $2.00
in 1942, and had a cash reserve of $12,000. (One of the stockholders
of Granada Theatre Company was A. B. Meydenbauer, an owner of
property east of Lake Washington in what would become Bellevue.)

John paid off the mortgage on the Palomar in 1943. Then, at
the end of 1944, the Third & University Corporation took out a new
loan against the Palomar and Garden Theatres for $450,000. John
was looking forward to expansion during peacetime, but not all of
his efforts came to fruition. He entered into a partnership with two
men who applied to the War Resources Board to build a new theater
in Lake City. The partnership was disbanded when the application
was turned down. He also purchased a lot on Granville Street in Vancouver, British Columbia, to build a theater. He gave up the project
because the City of Vancouver refused to allow the old building to
be torn down. It wasn't a bad deal in the end. He purchased the lot
on Granville for $95,000 in 1944 and sold it in 1949 for $175,000. He
then announced plans to build a new theater at Second and James
in downtown Seattle, but I don't believe this theater was ever built.

John was constantly involved in the civic life of the communities in which he operated theaters. He was a member of local
chambers of commerce, business roundtables, and fraternal and
service organizations.

❧ ✄

When a riot involving more than a hundred teens broke out on the
corner of 85th and Greenwood in Seattle (then at the city limits) in
January 1943, police and sheriff's deputies responded to the incident.
The neighborhood was moved to begin looking for an answer to the
overall issue of juvenile crime and vandalism, a growing problem in

the community. King County Sheriff's Deputy Joe Woelfert, with the support of many neighborhood merchants, opened the first Boys & Girls Club (originally called the Boys Club) in Washington State—the North Seattle Boys Club. The club was a great success, and within two years, eight clubs sprouted up in the area. John Danz was one of the first significant participants in the effort and remained involved with the Boys Clubs for much of his life.

Jessie also maintained a significant role in the community. As president of the board of directors of the Seattle Jewish Welfare Society, Jessie was busy planning the agency's fiftieth anniversary celebration to be held in March of 1942. This organization was the second oldest Community Fund agency in the region. The oldest was the Seattle Children's Home, where Jessie was a supporter and board member.

During the war years, many people worked two jobs, their own regular job and then a defense job. Bill and Fred each worked at Sterling during the day and then reported for the second shift, building bombers at Boeing. I remember the green lunch pail my dad took with him every morning in order to have a meal during his Boeing shift.

High schools recorded absenteeism among the older boys who could earn seventy-five cents an hour in a shipyard. Defense plants ran three shifts, leaving swing and graveyard workers with free time in the morning and afternoon. Often, the only recreation that people had was the movies. John met this transformation in sleep patterns with more showings and longer hours. In downtown Seattle during the war years, there were about six theaters that ran "all night," sort of. After the swing shift released workers at about midnight, thousands came downtown to see movies until two in the morning. Then they went to another movie until five. That left four hours to get the theater cleaned up and ready for patrons, many from the graveyard shift, at nine o'clock. After so many years of short and empty pay envelopes, people wanted to enjoy life. Of course, increasing the hours meant increased staffing, and John and his staff scrambled for good help, just like other businesses.

Throughout the war, John carried on a correspondence with several men in the service because he knew how important mail

JER 27, 1940 | VOL. XVII, No. 31

Officers and board members of the Seattle Jewish Welfare Society: Left to right: Mrs. A. M. Goldstein, vice president; Mrs. John Danz, president; Mrs. Roy Rosenthal, Community Fund representative; Mrs. Otto Guthman, secretary.

• • •   • • •

Seattle Jewish Women Devote Half Century Of Aid To Needy

With the opening of the 1940 Community Fund campaign only two days away, officers and board members of the Seattle Jewish Welfare Society, now in its 49th year of service to the Jewish community in Seattle, last week discovered their organization possesses the honor of being the second oldest fund agency.

Only the Seattle Childrens' Home, according to Mrs. John Danz, president, now surpasses the society in years of service, of all the 38 agencies associated with the Seattle Community Fund in the relief of suffering and want and the development of better, more useful citizens.

And today, according to Mrs. Danz, eight of the original charter members of the society, who on March 18, 1892, 49 years ago, held the first meeting, are still living in Seattle and the Northwest, and are actively interested in the work of the society. They are: Mrs. A. Lou Cohen, Mrs. J. Berkman, Mrs. Emmanuel Rosenberg, Mrs. Charles Roth, Mrs. I. Rosenthal, Mrs. E. Morgenstern, Mrs. J. R. Holmes and Mrs. Fred Bories.

Since the first meeting, the society has carried on a continuous program of social service in the Jewish community, working in close cooperation with other social service and character-building agencies under the Community Fund to relieve suffering

(Cont. on Page 8, Col. 1)

Jewish Welfare League
(Continued from Page 1)

teer workers, but with the growth of the city and the tremendous increase of work and the development of social consciousness and responsibility, a paid executive secretary was engaged and offices established in the Pacific Block. The Society continues to have a very large number of volunteer workers without whom the tremendous work accomplished by this organization would be impossible. Every member of the board does family visiting under the advisement of Miss May Goldsmith, the executive secretary. Many of the members do big sister work by concerning themselves with the problems of young girls, who require assistance.

When the Community Fund was organized the Seattle Hebrew Benevolent Society was one of the first organizations to join the group.

The present officers of the organization are: Mrs. John Danz, president; Mrs. H. Schneider, first vice-president; Mrs. Max Silver, third vice-president; Mrs. Henry Shopera, recording secretary; Mrs. Samuel Stern, corresponding secretary and Mrs. E. Silverstone, financial secretary. Mrs. M. Gerber, treasurer, and Miss May B. Goldsmith, executive secretary. The offices have moved from 507 Pacific Block to 408 Pacific Block.

The name of the society is linked with the name of the late Mrs. Therese Levy, who for twenty years served as its president.

Of the original charter members, the following are still here, and some are still active in the organization:

Mrs. S. Davis, Mrs. S. Aronson, Mrs. M. A. Gottstein, Mrs. I. Davis, Mrs. E. Rosenberg, Mrs. E. Morgenstern, Mrs. B. Roth, Mrs. E. Goodman, Mrs. A. Lou Cohen, Mrs. J. Berkman, Mrs. H. Elster, Mrs. I. Rosenthal, Mrs. Fred Bories, Mrs. I. Monheimer, Mrs. J. Marks, Mrs. E. C. Neufelder, Mrs. H. Lapworth, Mrs. John R. Holmes, Mrs. I. J. Lewis, Mrs. J. Selig, Mrs. Harold Preston and Mrs. Emil Lobe.

"In carrying on the work of our organization under a new name, we hope to preserve the intentions and carry on the wishes of the original founders, who recognized the need of caring for the Jewish poor efficiently," Mrs. Danz declared at the meeting. "We know that those progressive women who gave so generously of their time and energy in the old days would be among the first to take advantage of any change that would improve the conditions of those people whose well-being is in our trust."

Jessie planning Jewish Welfare Society 50th anniversary celebration. Left to Right Mrs. A. M. Goldstein, Mrs. John Danz, President, Mrs. Roy Rosenthal, Mrs. Otto Guthman
(Courtesy of Jewish Transcript)

from home was to the men. He also sent holiday gift packages every year. Some of these servicemen were friends of his children, some were children of his friends, some were relatives, and a few were former employees called into service. In April 1945, John wrote to Ted Kaufman, a cousin on the Suransky side, filling him in with the news from home. Among other things, he told Ted that a curfew had been put in place requiring all the theaters to close at midnight. He said, "That makes quite a difference in our receipts and of course the profits." However, he went on, business in general was even better than the previous year. In another letter that summer, he mentioned that the company had taken over three theaters and a couple of other buildings in Longview and Kelso. He had also entered into a pooling arrangement with Bill Forman, who was operating a theater in that region. He concluded by saying that "now we are friends and partners." John also informed Ted that Fred Danz had been called up by the navy and sent to San Diego to study radar.

John supported the war effort in many other ways: he contributed to the USO, donated passes to service personnel, loaned out some of the vaudeville talent he hired to entertain the troops at no charge to the men, opened up theaters for servicemen, and contributed in various ways to victory whenever asked.

The tens of thousands of people crowding into Seattle to take jobs at Boeing and others related to the war effort quickly consumed all available housing. During the Depression, there was almost no construction so the housing stock available in 1940 was often substandard and in short supply. Because the war economy gobbled up all available building materials, not much new housing went up that was not directly related to the war effort. People were happy to have jobs and accepted any place to lay their heads. Large, old homes in once-fashionable neighborhoods were cut up into apartments. Individual homeowners jury rigged basements and garages to take in renters. Workers on different shifts cooperated by renting the same apartment with the agreement that one slept while the other worked. Many workers just off shift had no empty beds to go home to so they spent a quarter for a movie. Some people used the all-night theaters as flophouses.

John's employees needed homes too. Late in the war, John found a partial solution to this problem when he purchased two apartment buildings, the Duchess and the Commodore on 15th Avenue (later 15th Avenue Northeast) in the University District. He wrote to the King County clerk that "on Saturday, February 17, 1945, I bought the Commodore Apartments for $201,000 at a sheriff's sale" and requested that he be sent the certificate of ownership. He used these buildings to provide decent housing for his higher-level employees. Throughout the war, he received letters from people moving to Seattle to take jobs at the university or in one of the many other active business ventures. Every letter requested special consideration in renting an apartment in his buildings. Some people even offered bribes. John replied personally and politely that the units were full and that he did not expect any vacancies soon. (These apartment houses were donated to the University of Washington upon John's death and became housing for married students.)

Commodore and Duchess Apartments.
(Post-Intelligencer Collection, Museum of History & Industry.)

John had to deal with another, much stranger, war shortage—popcorn seasoning and oil. He wrote letters to various places, including to suppliers in Canada, looking for a seasoning that tasted good. He was not very successful since everyone else in the movie business was confronted with the same shortages. Somehow, the movie-going public endured lower-quality popcorn for the duration of the conflict, but John was still dissatisfied that he could not provide the best.

On January 10, 1944, Louis Danz died after an illness of several months. His obituary says that he was born in 1850 and was ninety-four years old, but family records show his birth in 1852.

In 1945, John was honored at a banquet given by the Motion Picture Pioneers for his creative leadership as an independent exhibitor. Charles Reagan, vice president of Paramount Pictures, Inc., congratulating him on being one of the people being honored wrote, "You have helped to develop [our industry] from its infancy to the great business that it has become."

EXPANSION

❧ 1945–1950 ❧

With the defeat of the Axis and the end of the devastation and colossal loss of life, servicemen just wanted to get home, and everyone wanted to return to life as normal. People wanted to build new lives and spend money. Consumer demand, stifled by the Depression and then held in check by the need for tanks and planes, was released.

Despite the increase in consumer spending, business still faced many challenges. The country continued to experience shortages, particularly in housing. Servicemen came home to start families, and they wanted homes, cars, and appliances. John saw this as an opportunity to grow his business. In August of 1945, he wrote to a friend that he had plans to build several new theaters "as soon as materials and manpower are easier to obtain." He explored purchasing land in Victoria, British Columbia, for a theater but decided that it was too far from headquarters to manage efficiently.

From that time on, John sought new businesses to acquire that were within a day's trip of the head office so that the person from Seattle supervising the property and staff would not have to stay overnight for a visit. This is not surprising given that the company was run by a man who insisted on visiting every theater every evening after having dinner with his children. One of the first postwar additions was the

1945 purchase of the Longview Theatre in Longview, Washington, a facility the company continued to operate until May of 1955. The policy on distance that limited business acquisitions shifted some over time as cars, highways, and air transportation provided improved mobility, but the company today still focuses on properties within a day's journey. Most locations are reachable with a reasonable drive or flight, and the choice to stay over or return home the same day is left to the property manager.

Longview Theatre, 1945.

There was one significant exception to this practice. Jessie's sister Lillian and her family had moved to California in the early 1920s, where about fifteen years later their daughter Frances met and married Matt Appelman (born in 1910 in today's Belarus). Fran met Matt at a meeting of the Young Communist League in Los Angeles, probably while she was either still in high school or in her first year of college. They married in 1936, and their son Dan writes:

> Dad was first a union organizer after high school, organizing mine workers in Kentucky, Tennessee and Los Angeles. He was also an organizer for the American Communist Party and was Secretary of the ACP in Los Angeles when he met Fran.

Matt became uncomfortable with the control that the Soviet Union imposed on the Communist parties worldwide, its intolerance of divergent viewpoints, and its treatment of American Communists who differed from the party line. But even more, he felt he could no longer be a Communist when he learned what Stalin had done to various ethnic and national groups (including Jews) and to his political opponents within the Soviet Union.

Dan thinks Matt went into the army in 1940 or 1941 when he was about thirty. While he was serving with the U.S. Army in Germany, helping to liberate prisoners from concentration camps, Fran and their infant son, Dan, lived with Joe and Lilly in Pacoima. Dan tells me that he was about a year old when his dad came home in late 1945 or early 1946.

Matt Appelman.

Matt Appelman didn't have any immediate job prospects as a civilian so John, always one to help family, asked Matt to help him find property for a movie theater in Southern California. Matt found a spot in Pasadena and built the Hastings Drive-In Theatre under John's guidance and tutelage. The theater opened in 1948 and according to Dan:

> Once the theater was built, Dad managed it, learned to buy films from the distributors, and began to look for other locations for theaters in Southern California. I think John was open to expanding [Sterling] from the Pacific Northwest to Southern California, which was a growing population center, and Dad was available, willing to learn, and smart. One way to look at it was that John was looking out for family and offering us an opportunity when Dad had no immediate prospects of supporting his family otherwise. Another way of looking at it was that he found in Dad someone who could help him expand and grow [Sterling] beyond what it could be as it was then, and to make [Sterling] more profitable. I'm sure both were true. The next project started soon after the Hastings opened with the purchase of land in Santa Fe Springs and the opening of the La Mirada Drive-In Theatre in 1952.

Hastings Drive-In Theatre, Pasadena, California, built 1947.

Grand opening of La Mirada Theater with Rose Parade Band.

I am also sure both were true. Anyone who wasn't capable, loyal, smart, and creative didn't work long for John. Matt built quite a significant presence for the Sterling chain in the region. According to Tad Danz, one of John's three grandsons, the theaters were known along Film Row in Los Angeles as the Appelman Theaters, although they were officially the California Sterling Theatres. These theaters were not really part of Sterling Theatres. California Sterling Theatres was an entity wholly owned by Jessie and John. Bookkeeping, film buying, and all other operations were independent of the organization in the Northwest.

Meanwhile, the theater chain in the Northwest expanded eastward. In 1940, the state of Washington completed a floating bridge from Seattle, across Mercer Island, to the east side of Lake Washington. The "Eastside" began growing into a bedroom community, very slowly during the war years and more quickly after 1945. Instead of riding the streetcar to work, people drove automobiles so that they could live in outlying towns and keep their jobs in town. When cars became widely available again after the war, people snapped them up. Homes and home sites outside the Seattle city limits grew in popularity.

In Bellevue, where downtown was then just a post office, there was little convenient shopping available for the new residents until 1946, when developer Kemper Freeman, Sr., opened Bellevue Shopping Square with a Frederick & Nelson department store as the anchor. Even before the war's end, Freeman managed to convince government officials to let him build a movie theater as a morale booster. On March 20, 1946, the first business to open in the new shopping center was Sterling's 550-seat Bel-Vue Theatre (the theater continued in operation until 1981).

As the company expanded, communications between management, managers, and staff became more critical. John created *The Spotlight*, a weekly newsletter, originally containing information about monthly contests and tips on keeping the theaters spotless, then later expanded to include biographies of new staff, reminders, and company news. Every quarter there was at least one contest for all theater managers and their staff. Sometimes the ideas for the contests came from managers' suggestions, but most of the time the ideas came from John, Fred, or another of the executives. When Zollie Volchok joined the company, he generated many new ideas for contests.

In 1946, there was a Service Award Contest in which theater managers and their staffs were judged on the quality of their service to the patrons, such as courtesy, attitude, deportment, personal appearance, efficiency, and reliability. Prizes included a plaque awarded to the theater for display in the lobby and dinner for the entire theater staff.

Convinced that customers responded to good service, John and the company instituted a quarterly Honor Award for outstanding courtesy to the patrons. These contests served many purposes—helping to reinforce various company standards and guidelines, supporting the efforts of the managers to build a cohesive team within each theater, and rewarding employees for making an effort to excel. The contests also helped to identify weak managers or employees who just didn't meet the standards John and his company tried to maintain.

One competition, called the Aspirin Contest, dealt with headache-inducing problems in the theaters that were the responsibility of each theater's manager. Inter-office messages from the office to the theaters

Sterling Theatres Annual Managers Meeting, December 15, 1948, Olympic Hotel.
Fred Danz is standing at left. Starting third from left are Bill Danz, John Danz,
and Zollie Volchok .

pointed out any issues discovered by John's men during their nightly visits to the theaters plus accounting questions, reports from personnel or patron complaints. Managers reported film issues—scratched or poor-quality film, late arrivals, wrong trailers, etc.—problems with concessions, staffing, maintenance, and such. Each issue received points in the form of aspirin icons. A simple issue could rate one aspirin, increasing to three aspirins for the most serious cases. The manager with the fewest aspirins in a quarter won the contest.

Another contest involved the amount of seasonings used on the popcorn. Popcorn seasoning was fairly expensive. The winning theater popped precisely fifty pounds of corn per pound of seasoning used! The average for all theaters was about 16.5 pounds of corn per pound of seasoning.

Reminders to managers included tidbits such as:

Cashiers should not give silver dollars to customers as change unless they have no paper money. Patrons do not like the heavy coins in their pockets.

Please be a little more attentive to your doorman's appearance. Ragged shirts, worn out ties and un-shined shoes certainly detract from the otherwise attractiveness of a theatre.

Cleaning tips were a regular part of *The Spotlight*, including the following:

The glass on all suburban marquees is to be washed down every time the letters are changed. There is no excuse for a dirty marquee.

How do you keep a popcorn kettle clean? Manager Charles Leaming has a strange formula. [Alas, the formula has eluded my research.]

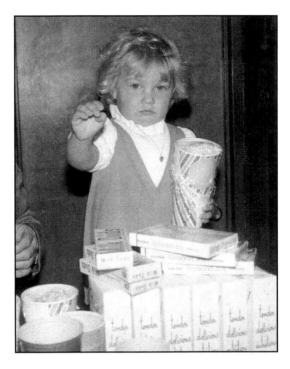

Mmmmm, popcorn.

Theaters used a great many advertising devices, what John called "exploitation." They arranged tie-ins with stores and organizations in their neighborhoods to do giveaways and contests for Mother's Day and other holiday events. One week, patrons received umbrellas. Another week, managers held drawings for a gift certificate from a local store or a chance to win a set of dishes or pots and pans (John was not happy when one of the drawings was for a set of dishes that was not associated with any of the local merchants).

In one issue, *The Spotlight* featured Winfield "Bill" Kennedy who started as a doorman at the Colonial Theatre in 1922, became the assistant manager, and then manager. In 1934, he became a projectionist, a highly responsible job since viewers had no patience with broken film, lamps burning out, and other technical difficulties. Then, as now, moviegoers insisted on a flawless performance. Bill Kennedy retired in 1947 after twenty-five years with the company. All was reported in *The Spotlight*.

In 1946, the average worker's salary was $150 a month. After thirty years, he could expect to receive retirement checks of $58.50 a month from Social Security.

Many changes occurred during 1946. Children's matinees, which had begun the year before in Milwaukee, proved to be so successful that they spread to other cities. These matinees were heavily promoted with a variety of schemes. There were giveaways of comic books, paper games, and bubble gum. (Theater owners learned quickly to give out the gum only as the children left the theaters.) There were fun events, including cracker-eating contests, bubble-gum-blowing derbies (again, caution dictated that gum be given to contestants only), and pie-eating competitions. Door prizes and drawings were frequent gimmicks that kept the kids coming back week after week. There was even the occasional drawing for a bicycle.

Our family lived on lower Capitol Hill. As children, my sisters and I spent almost every Saturday in the late forties with our friends at the Roycroft Theatre at 19th and Roy. Two cartoons, a serial, the news of the week, and a family-oriented feature film marked the end of our week in school. Daddy gave us each a quarter for the movies. It cost ten cents for the ticket, a nickel for a Coke, a nickel for popcorn and a nickel for a Hershey Bar. Heaven every Saturday. According to one of the neighborhood kids on Queen Anne, they called their theater "the Dink."

Not everyone approved of the Saturday afternoon serials. In September 1946, John received a letter from the members of a West Seattle group complaining that, "It is our contention that the serial is unwholesome, that it has a corruptive influence on the children … and that its continued display is detrimental." John always responded personally to these concerns and a great many of the other issues that were brought to his attention.

One man wrote to John with an objection that a young woman was working in the theater at the "menial task of cleaning up paper cups, chewing gum wrappers, Kleenex, popcorn, etc., during the inter-mission period." John responded that he had investigated thoroughly, that the young woman was happy to have the job, that the work was appropriate for a young woman to do, and that it was intended to help keep the theater clean.

He wrote notes to patrons, returning their lost sweater, wallet, identification, or jewelry, reprimanded managers for an un-swept sidewalk, and sent theater passes to assuage angry customers who felt abused in some way. Here is one of my personal favorites: "We have in our possession a sword which you lost in the Winter Garden Theatre."

Sterling had grown to the point that it began operating its own delivery service for things like film pick-ups, popcorn, seasoning, and advertising from the "Row." Film Row was a two-block section in downtown Seattle that housed a screening theater, distribution companies, and a variety of other motion-picture related businesses. The Row even merited its own regular gossip column in the *Seattle Times*.

The company expanded again with the opening of the Lincoln and Olympian theaters in Olympia, Washington, well within the one-day travel limit.

Lincoln Theatre.

❧ Humanism ❧

Sometime around the middle of the 1940s, John was introduced to the humanist movement. Humanism at the time focused on benevolence through the use of reason, ethics, and justice while rejecting reliance on the supernatural and on organized religious dogma. Despite his Jewish background, John had a strong antipathy towards religion of all kinds and to any system that provided services only to parts of the community. Although he was a man of deep convictions and faith, he believed each person should depend upon himself for aid, improvements, and guidance—not an unusual stance for a self-made man. He believed man could be kind, generous, compassionate, fair, and honorable in his relations with his fellow man.

He also felt that organizations that made decisions based on race or religion were detrimental and divisive. In 1948, he wrote to the chairman of the Membership Campaign of the National Conference of Christians and Jews, an organization he had supported for many years:

> Inasmuch as your organization gives forth the impression of being concerned with only two classes of peoples in this world—Christians and Jews—leaving the balance of the human race to be intimidated in an inharmonious world, I do not feel that I can again renew my membership.

The following year he responded to an invitation to attend the Northwest Regional Conference of the Joint Defense Appeal.

> For many years, probably thirty or more, I was a member of the B'nai B'rith for only one reason—the anti-defamation part of their activities. On account of my recent affiliation with the Humanists I resign from the B.B. However, I am still very much interested in anti-defamation for all races, colors, and creeds.

He wrote to prominent persons, such as poet and writer Archibald MacLeish, who he thought were of a liberal bent and asked if he could meet with them. To actor/director Walter Huston, he penned,

I am planning to spend a few days in New York and would like to meet you and have you give me an hour or so of your time to take up a matter pertaining to a liberal movement … I consider we are mutually interested in [this issue] as a result of seeing the short [feature] you were in with Aimee Semple McPherson.[2]

John wrote to Jessie's brother George that he would be in Chicago

attending a convention of the American Humanist Association, of which I am a member, and about which I will go into detail when I see you … Humanism is the religion that I heard about on one of my trips to New York, and determined, after investigation, that it came nearest to my idea of a transcended religion.

He asked his sister-in-law Freda, executive director of Jewish Family Service in Los Angeles, to try to locate people connected to the humanist movement. She responded with information about Dr. Lowell N. Coate of Los Angeles and Fred Shorter of the Church of the People in the University District in Seattle. He also discovered, however, a strong antagonism towards the humanist movement from many of the Unitarian ministers in Los Angeles. Eventually John purchased a building in which to house the Humanist Society in Los Angeles at 6128 Selma Avenue. He also purchased a house on Jackson Street in San Francisco for use by the local Humanist Society.

This introduction to the humanist movement would affect many of John's decisions and relationships for the rest of his life. He traveled to meet people in the movement, to hear prominent speakers, and to learn as much as he could about the issues. He became the primary supporter of humanism in the Pacific Northwest and was, for a time, deeply involved in the humanist movement in the Los Angeles and San Francisco Bay areas.

Travel by air was a great time saver in the 1940s but by our standards was very arduous, and John was already in his sixties. A flight from Seattle to Washington, D.C., aboard a four-engine DC-6

---

2   Evangelist of the 1920s and 1930s and an early media celebrity.

took about seventeen hours—leaving Seattle at five in the evening, stopping in Chicago at six the next morning, and arriving in D.C. at noon.

❧ ❧

In the navy training camp, Fred met Zalmon Marcola "Zollie" Volchok of Portland. The entertainment business in the Pacific Northwest was a fairly small fraternity, so they had heard of each other but had never met. Zollie had been in show business most of his life, starting with a radio program as a child in Salem, Oregon. He told me that when he was thirteen he started the first Mickey Mouse Club in the United States. He wrote a column in the paper every week in the 1930s called "Mickey Mouse Notes," which he continued all through college. His senior year he worked for the University of Oregon helping with events. The first attraction he ever booked was Paul Whiteman for one of the proms. Then he booked a very famous banjo player named Eddy Peabody. Zollie said that Peabody wrote in his book about a young kid who introduced him on stage by saying "Eddy Playbody will now Pee for you." Zollie was managing the Fox theaters in Portland when he was drafted. Fred and Zollie got to be friends before Fred shipped out for occupation duty in Japan. After returning home from the Navy, Fred spoke to John about Zollie, and John set out to hire him away from Portland. John Danz was attentive not only to new business opportunities but also to promising talent for his company.

John went to Portland and approached Zollie about working for Sterling. Zollie said he wasn't interested. By the time John returned to Portland, with a lawyer in tow, Zollie had already contacted other men who had worked for John and told John, "You are just too tough to work for." According to Zollie, John "laid down a piece of paper with figures on it—which was double what I was making. It was a lot of money in those days." John also offered him free rent for a year in a house on Lake Washington. "I said, 'Mr. Danz, you can be as tough on me as you want.'" Zollie accepted the offer and moved to Seattle with his wife, Sylvia, in August of 1946.

The following spring, just a few months into his contract, Jessie asked Sylvia when they were going to move out. Jessie had urged

John to purchase the house in Madison Park as a lakeside retreat from May Goldsmith, executive director of the Jewish Family and Child Service (later Jewish Family Service) on whose board of directors Jessie served for several decades. The purchase closed in February of 1946, so this would be the first summer Jessie would have the opportunity to relax there with her grandchildren and children and their spouses. Of course, Jessie had not heard about the arrangement between John and Zollie.

Sylvia called Zollie on the phone, distraught. Jessie wanted them out of the house the next week. Fred was in John's office when Zollie came in. As Zollie told the story, he asked John,

> What's this all about? John said, "Well you know I told you, you could stay there for a while." I said, "Read my contract," and I walked out. Fred came running to my office on the floor above. He said, "Find any place to live for the rest of the seven months and we'll pay for it. John doesn't have to know about it." So we took a home in West Seattle on Beach Drive—right on the water. We slept twenty-eight people, to give you an idea. We stayed there for five years till we moved to Lake Washington Boulevard. But I always remember that when I think about John.

By May, Jessie arranged to have the yard of the old house in Madison Park landscaped and made ready for her family to enjoy throughout the summer.

❧ ❧

The end of the war signaled the beginning of the end of vaudeville in Sterling Theatres. When John refused to increase performers' salaries in 1945, Sterling went on the "unfair" list of the American Guild of Variety Artists. Between the difficulties he experienced with the AGVA and the problems he had had with the Musicians Union in the twenties and thirties, John finally decided to move to a pictures-only policy in most of his theaters. John wrote to a colleague that the musicians had forced the elimination of vaudeville at the Palomar and the rest of Seattle by raising the minimum hours and wage higher than during the war, meaning that John would have to pay each musician more per hour for more hours each week. On January 1, 1946, they raised it further. He pointed out that the musicians had made concessions in many other cities throughout the country and hoped that the Seattle union would "see the light." For a time in 1946, there was no vaudeville in any of John's theaters.

He continued to negotiate and reinstated vaudeville for several years, but only at the Palomar. Zollie explained that people had gotten tired of vaudeville acts. There would be a dancer, a singer, a juggler, and maybe a magician. Zollie changed Sterling's booking policy and started bringing in the best acts in the country to perform in Seattle as concerts. The first one was Mel Torme. Over the years, he brought in other big names: Nat King Cole, the Andrews Sisters, the Will Masten Trio (Sammy Davis Jr. with his father and uncle), jazz pianist Earl Hines, Louis Armstrong, and Victor Borge. Several of these performers played as many as eight years in a row.

Zollie Volchok with Victor Borge.

Jazz Pianist Earl Hines

The Andrews Sisters

Louis Armstrong with Esquire Awards
earned 1942-47

The Palomar hosted its final vaudeville performance, starring Sammy Davis Jr., in 1953. Zollie said,

> The Palomar was one of the last [to host vaudeville], one of the first, and it was the last. There were two left that we knew of: the Orpheum Theatre in Los Angeles and the Palomar. When we were doing five a day, we used to exchange. [The Orpheum] closed up first, and after I left [Sterling], they stopped vaudeville at the Palomar.

❦

African American entertainers like Sammy Davis, Jr., Louis Armstrong, and Nat King Cole were wonderfully received by the audiences, but outside the theater, things were different. In the 1940s, housing and public accommodations in Seattle were unofficially segregated or restricted. Hotel operators could discriminate for any reason, including race. Most Seattle homeowners' deeds contained restrictive covenants against selling to Asians, African Americans, and Jews. Nor were they welcome in the exclusive gated communities of Broadmoor and Sand Point, the Seattle Tennis Club, the Seattle Athletic Club, or the country clubs. The covenant written into the deeds of Broadmoor, for example, read:

> No part of said property hereby conveyed shall ever be used or occupied by any Hebrew or by any person of the Ethiopian, Malay or any Asiatic Race … excepting only employees in the domestic service on the premises of persons qualified hereunder as occupants and users and residing on the premises.

The Olympic Hotel, the premier hostelry and social venue in Seattle, was happy to provide lodging for the headliners brought in to town by Sterling, as long as they were white. John solved the problem, according to Zollie, by purchasing the Savoy Hotel at Occidental Avenue South and South Main Street, near where Occidental Park is now.

The hotel housing barrier was not broken until late in the forties or early fifties. Zollie had booked the Ink Spots into the Paramount, and according to Zollie, they were one of the biggest attractions around. Zollie got a call from Bill Kenney, the main singer in the Ink Spots. Kenney said he needed a favor. He had just married a white girl, and her parents were going to meet them in Seattle. He wanted them all to be able to stay at the Olympic Hotel. Zollie met with Thomas A. Gildersleve, the manager of the Olympic.

> I told him that this is ridiculous. In Portland we're now able to put them in the Benson. Here we have a gentleman with a very big band. He compromised and let him stay there with his wife and her family. The rest of the group stayed at the Savoy. But it broke the barrier. Later on when Ella Fitzgerald came in and then Don Ho who was so big in Hawaii, we were able to put them in the major hotels.

Theaters were segregated, as well, but more subtly. In those days, most theater patrons were ushered to their seats, and John's instructions, particularly at the Palomar, were that the blacks should be seated on one side of the house. John thought that's what people wanted, and he was not far off the mark. In 1955, there was an incident at the Roosevelt Theatre. The accident report from the theater manager states:

> On May 29 Mrs. Gladys M__ claimed to have been pushed by a colored girl while coming out of the Restroom and sustained a sprained ankle. Mrs. M__ expressed her desire to have the girl who pushed her arrested, and I told her I would get a policeman for her if she wanted, but that it would just be her word against the girls [*sic*]. She then said that she certainly would not come back to the Roosevelt Theatre again, and I asked her if she considered it our fault. She said, "no," but that she didn't think that colored people should be allowed in the same theatre as white. I

told her that we couldn't discriminate against people and that we couldn't take sides in the matter.

Housing discrimination and segregation in public accommodations formally ended in Seattle in the late 1960s.

❧ ❧

John always had a vision and a plan. It was always in the back of his mind—the company was going to be bigger. He talked to his managers about needing a theater in a particular neighborhood or wanting to build better, more interesting and elegant houses. He wanted to expand into the new areas like the east side of Lake Washington. And he often talked about investing in land. Any time he had a profit at the end of the year, he invested in more real estate. The landless peasant from Bryansk who was thrown out of Russia was always looking for land. Zollie told me that John often advised him to use any extra money to invest in real estate, and Zollie added he wishes he had paid better attention to that advice.

He also looked to expand into the smaller cities and towns. But it was often difficult for an outsider to come in to a tight community like Longview or Port Angeles to establish a business, so John often entered a market by creating a partnership with an existing business that needed capital.

In 1947, the Far West Company declared a dividend of $15,000, and John expanded again. As was to become his pattern, he formed a partnership with an existing company in Port Angeles that was experiencing financial problems. In December 1946, John wrote to the National Theater Supply Company, informing them that he had an option to purchase one half of the business owned by the Halbergs in Port Angeles and intended to exercise that option. "The cash payment attendant to this transaction will permit full settlement of your account."

Port Angeles Theater.

However, bringing an existing business under John's exacting management style created some problems, and John fired off frequent memos to partner Ed Halberg. There was an issue with a cashier filling out her statements before closing, probably so she could go home early. But when people bought tickets after her report was completed, the report was no longer accurate. Since the distributors and the production companies were paid by the number of tickets sold, there was the potential of lost revenue. The distributor complained and raised the issue of cheating. Such problems might affect future negotiations for films in that theater or even in the entire chain.

In one note to Halberg, John complained about the expense of decorating one of the Port Angeles theaters for the holidays. Instead of paying one of the ushers or janitors to do it, or doing it himself, the manager had assigned the task to one of the operators, a more highly paid employee earning $1.65 per hour. John informed Halberg that in many of the theaters, the manager and his family took great delight in doing this task themselves [at no cost to the theater].

When John learned that the marquee was not being lit immediately at nightfall, he sent a memo clarifying policy and reinforcing earlier instructions.

One of the frequent general reminders to theater managers was this admonition: "Be sure to spray your popcorn & candy rooms with a good moth killer each week." Mouse infestations were also a problem in almost every theater.

After Bill Forman left Sterling in 1940, he built a drive-in theater in Tacoma. In 1946, he founded United States Drive-In Theatres. In mid-1948, he entered into an agreement to take over two theaters still being constructed by a California company called Pacific Drive-In Theatres, Inc., the Van Nuys and the Lakewood, for $103,174. John and Sterling were partners with Bill as he began to build this business, providing both the original $103,174, which was a loan from Sterling to United, and an additional $73,538, the full amount of outstanding invoices due on the two new drive-in theaters still under construction. When Bill built the Duwamish Drive-In Theatre, John had a piece since it was built on John's land just south of Boeing Field. It opened in May 1948, just in time for the summer.

Bill Forman

❧ ❧

Fred, Bill, and Zollie—"the boys"—shared the responsibility of nightly visits to the theaters. Of course, they never knew when John was going to show up or where since he never stopped making his own nightly visits. With three trusted young executives, John was able to increase his managerial wingspan and operate a larger number of venues. Their written reports included the appropriateness of the staffing levels, given the size of the house (number of patrons), and included both positive and negative issues. Comments included the cleanliness of the theater, the appearance and behavior of the staff (talking, snacking, or not paying attention), and suggestions for improvements of various kinds (a new toilet seat, other repairs and maintenance needed, lights out on the marquee or interior lighting). Even the popcorn bags—under- or over-filled—received scrutiny and comment.

The company augmented the regular, personal site visits with a shopper's service to report on the operation of the theaters. Secret shoppers visited theaters and bowling centers posing as regular patrons to see how managers and employees behaved when the bosses weren't around. The inspectors' reports included a wide variety of issues, reporting both positive and negative findings. In late 1947, one theater received an excellent report and another, a fairly negative one. In the latter circumstance, the stairway and foyer were filled with popcorn and candy wrappers, and the theater was very noisy. The doorman didn't watch the door, and the men's room was dirty, having not been cleaned once between eight and ten thirty in the evening.

Another secret shopper found one of the large admission signs lying face down on the sidewalk, no one on the door taking tickets, and plenty of visiting in the box office by both employees and patrons. The shopper even missed part of the dialogue during the film because of conversation between the ushers and their friends. I can only imagine John's reaction to this series of deficiencies.

Communication went in both directions. Managers reported every week about their theaters. They knew what John wanted to know: How did the Saturday matinee go? Did the films show up on time? Were they in good condition when they were shown? Managers occasionally complained about the scratches on the cartoon print or the poor quality of the sound track.

Managers' reports documented how the new giveaway was received or the level of participation in the contest of the week. Was Keno (a game with prizes) successful? Did anyone win the big prize? The stage drape is in bad shape. The phone company wants to install a pay booth in the lobby. What local area merchant tie-ins had been accomplished or were being planned for the near future? Several of the reports I read were from John's brother Simon who managed the Winter Garden Theatre at 1515 Third Avenue between Pine and Pike.

From the very beginning, John had insisted that his theaters be the best they could be. Zollie said, when he joined the company as district manager, excellence was simply part of the organization's rules. To maintain this standard, Zollie's theater checks always included one phase of operation that he went over personally with the manager. He asked each to have a suggestion for improvement of that area ready for his visit. Constantly striving to improve was the norm at Sterling.

One of Zollie's notes to the manager of the Queen Anne and Uptown theaters requested that she "arrange to have one of [the] boys paint the disposal receptacle ... near the popcorn machine." Another mentioned that the main feature trailer had run after the second picture's trailer and the policy was that the main feature trailer must run first. A third memo to a different manager mentioned broken glass in a picture on the wall of the men's room. No detail was too small to mention, and nothing was left to chance. Deficiencies were ignored at the manager's hazard.

❦ ❧

In November 1948, the Magnolia Theatre opened with a gala grand opening night. It was one of the most elegant neighborhood movie houses in Seattle. Murals of magnolia blossoms and carved panels of stylized flowers in bloom decorated the theater. The house featured a new no-glare screen, push-back seats, high-fidelity sound, a cry- ing room for families with infants, and an illuminated parking area.

Magnolia Creators, left to right: John H. Sellen, contractor;
John Danz; A. B. Heinsbergen, designer;
B. Marcus Priteca, architect.

At the grand opening celebration, John gave a speech, talking about the values of a family theater and the education and pleasure people receive from going for a night out at the movies. The response from the public can be summed up in this letter from a local resident.

I just wanted to write a word of appreciation for the splendid and dignified way in which the Magnolia Theater is being conducted. I think that you have added something that is needed in helping to keep our young people here in our own area and I personally appreciate the high level on which you have run the theater.

Entrance to Magnolia Theatre auditorium.

In November 1948, daylight-saving time became official in the Seattle area. The idea was anathema to operators of drive-in theaters, especially in the northern states where it stays light in the summer until quite late. Hours of darkness are the most profitable time for drive-in operation. John actively battled to defeat the proposition, but the time change became the law. The drive-in theaters were affected greatly, but John stuck with the business. In October of 1949, he worked up a plan to build a drive-in theater in Longview, Washington, on fifteen acres along 15th Avenue, south of the Ocean Beach Highway. He failed to get the zoning changed to accommodate a theater, but he continued to pursue other options for a drive-in in the area. He finally built the Longview Drive-In in 1950 on a different parcel of land. That same year he succeeded in building the Port Angeles Drive-In Theatre at a cost of $7,600 on a twenty-acre site on which his Port Angeles partner, Ed Halberg, had obtained an option.

❧ ❧

The structure of the company in the late forties had John as the president, Fred as CEO and head of the booking department, and Bill as treasurer and head of accounting and finance. Zollie was the district manager and directly responsible for the operation of the theaters and bowls. Zollie recalls that there were about ten to twelve people in the head office at that time. John made the final decision about whether to build or not. Bill's responsibility was to work out the financing, and he didn't usually get involved in the regular day-to-day operations of the company. Zollie and Fred had that responsibility and would discuss the various issues amongst themselves. If there was a problem they couldn't settle, they would take it to John for his input. Hiring and firing of the operating unit staff was up to Zollie, but if John developed a dislike for a particular employee, you can be sure that he or she was quickly gone. On the other hand, he valued and recognized loyalty and excellence. Employees who met the standards were often employed for decades and some for their entire careers.

John, Fred, and Zollie often received and responded to letters from theater customers, some with criticism and some with compliments. When a patron complained about her treatment at the Palomar, Zollie responded that a staff meeting had been held and the "usherettes were admonished for failure to uphold the standards of service which we have set for our theatres." Zollie enclosed two passes for her to use as a guest of the company.

Fred responded to a complaint that two young men were embarrassed by having to pay full adult admission prices with an apology and two passes. He sent another apologetic explanation to a man who complained about a vaudeville emcee who was not up to par. Another appreciative response went to a letter complimenting him on the revival attractions that were being shown in one of the theaters.

Zollie's relationship with John was complicated. John respected Zollie's skills and expertise and trusted him more and more. Zollie proved he could run the theaters and the bowling centers at the level John wanted. However, they definitely had differences of opinion in many areas.

> He'd say, "You really should change your name." And I'd say, "How about Zol Vol?" John would get angry and shout, "Don't make fun of me!"

Zollie also described the time when the Northgate Theatre opened in 1952. Zollie was inspecting the theater with the architect/ designer Anthony B. Heinsbergen and noticed that there was no mirror in the lobby.

> I said, "You have to put a mirror in." He said, "No, it will spoil the decorations." I said, "John Danz will want a mirror in there because he always wants a mirror." Heinsbergen thought John wouldn't say anything because it was a beautiful place and a mirror would just spoil the design.

The men made a twenty-five cent bet over whether or not John would want a mirror. Zollie went on to say,

> They were taking pictures of the opening with executives of the Northgate Mall when John Danz turns around and says, "There's no mirror in here." Heinsbergen reached over and handed me a quarter. John says, "What was that?" I said, "I bet him a quarter that you would want a mirror.

Nothing more was said until the next day when John confronted Zollie angrily,

> How I embarrassed him. The first time he ever bawled me out. We had disagreed on things many times, but in a manner that was peaceful. He really gave it to me. "I'm going to hold up your bonus!" (He didn't.)

❧ ❧

The cost of booking films was a recurring issue through the years that the organization stayed in the motion picture business. In 1947, Fred wrote to John, "No matter what we pay for film rental we cannot show a profit." Films were rented on a sliding scale according to the gross at each theater. In the same letter, however, Fred reminded John that "first weeks' sliding scale are not supposed to go below 25%." He went on that "we had not needed a scale below the 25% point and Mr. Walton said when we needed the lower percentage figures he would take care of us." When Fred spoke to the distributor about it, "he absolutely refused to submit the adjustment to Walton." Fred then requested that John handle the issue while he was still in New York. Month after month, year after year, there were dozens of letters to the distributors and within the company about the problems associated with the rental rates for good pictures throughout the circuit.

Another letter explained that Sterling was not even attempting to rent films from Fox because the studio insisted on renting a percentage of films booked into the theater in Kelso, an arrangement that was just not going to turn a profit. Another time they felt that RKO had not been fair on a particular film group and would not refund any of the excess payments. John responded by not renting RKO's block of films. Then there was a problem with *The Al Jolson Story* showing in Longview along with a whole series of issues concerning the MGM distributors in the rest of the Portland district (The Dalles, Kelso, and Longview). All of this was before the Paramount Decision came down in 1948. The fight for decent rates for independent exhibitors was continuous.

The Depression served to clean out weak and marginal theaters, and it stimulated the establishment of national circuits, "block booking," and "cross licensing." Block booking required that an exhibitor buy an entire year's product from a film producer without seeing the pictures. John was asked to buy pictures that were titles only on the assurance that they would be hits. John refused to participate in block booking. He did the best he could to ensure not only that his customers received a clean and cheerful experience but also that the film they paid to see was the best that he could offer.

Cross-licensing was when film companies who owned theaters would license the films that they produced to other chains owned by other distributors or producers. An independent exhibitor like John who had neither a distribution network nor a production company was unable to compete for films that were licensed under that methodology. This practice triggered a lawsuit by the U.S. Department of Justice on behalf of Midwest independent exhibitors alleging restraint of trade. The 1948 Paramount Decision forced the major film companies to either sell their theaters or sell the studios, to quit cross licensing, and to stop selling films on a block basis. Films were then sold on an individual basis.

This was a great stimulus to the independent exhibitor. They were able to move much more quickly than the big circuits and establish themselves in the new markets that emerged after World War II. As the studios divested themselves of their theaters, there was more opportunity for exhibitors like John to expand their chains in their existing markets as well as in new cities.

The exhibitors that had perpetrated the conditions that ended with the Paramount Decision thought that they were the white knights that had saved the industry. They found that when the studios no longer had responsibility to keep films in their own theaters, the studios reduced their production tremendously. When a studio owned theaters, producers had to complete their pictures to meet scheduled exhibition dates. Studios operated on strict industrial schedules. Ronald Reagan quipped about his years in the studio system, "They didn't want it good, they wanted it Thursday." There was a tremendous drop in the number of films being produced, starting in the late 1940s and early 1950s. But the films that came out were of increasing quality.

By 1947, John operated twenty-five theaters and a few apartment houses. Adult tickets at the Woodland Theatre were fifty cents, and candy was selling for five or ten cents. The cost to the theaters for candy was 20 to 30 percent of the selling price.

Woodland Theatre, Northwest 65th Street and Sixth Avenue Northwest, 1949.

Near the end of the decade, the business climate turned yet again. Revenues had fallen by about 20 percent, not only in Seattle but also in the suburbs and smaller communities. Wartime wage controls created an expectation of wage increases among American workers. When management balked, union members struck. President Harry Truman threatened to draft striking railroad workers into the army if they didn't go back to work. Naturally, workers on strike did not tend to go to the movies, and John's business suffered every time there was a walkout. In 1948, John commented in a letter to a colleague about strikes at Tacoma lumber mills and at the Boeing Company.

> The streets are practically empty of shoppers. People are certainly clamming down on their money. A good example of the local theatre business was on Tuesday nite [sic] last when I stood on the corner of Ninth and Broadway where I could observe all three of the theaters, Rialto, Music Box and Roxy. In a half an hour there was [sic] exactly three people went into any of the various houses.

On the positive side, the wartime building ban for amusement and entertainment buildings was finally lifted, providing the opportunity for John to build the Magnolia in 1948 and begin planning the Northgate Theatre to be opened in 1951.

John was no longer able to remain anonymous. His business dealings were reported in the papers and noticed by the rest of the community. In March 1948, Mr. Faragher, vice chairman of the National Bank of Commerce, noticed the purchase of the Longview Theater by the Sterling chain. He sent John a letter assuring him that NBC had the best banking facilities in Longview. He also commented that he thought John had "taken the pledge" not to take over any additional theaters. John responded somewhat humorously that, while he had at one time been hesitant to expand, "I overcame the uncertainty when I perceived your organization acquiring bank after bank. I considered it my duty to keep up as much as possible the example shown by your institution." Besides, as he pointed out, the purchase did not add another theater to the chain. Sterling had been operating it for several years. Also, the Longview Theatre had been banking with the Longview branch of NBC for all of those years, as had Sterling's three other theaters in Longview and Kelso.

Despite the business doldrums, the movies did well. On February 15, 1949, the Admiral Theatre posted the all-time high gross for a week of $3,560 for *The Best Years of our Lives*, starring Myrna Loy, Fredric March, and Dana Andrews. The drama traced the experiences of returning servicemen and their families and won the Academy Award for Best Picture in 1948.

Then on April 13, 1949, an estimated 7.1 magnitude earthquake struck western Washington and lasted for thirty seconds. Eight people, including two children, died under collapsed buildings and fallen walls. Bricks fell, foundations and walls cracked, and ceilings fell in. Some of John's buildings sustained significant damage. Repairs had to come out of company accounts since insurance did not cover earthquake damage. Some buildings, like the Circle Theatre and the Commodore and Duchess Apartments across the street from the University of Washington, required significant investment from a business already strapped for cash.

Earthquake damage on Second Avenue, Seattle, April 13, 1949. Florence Theatre in background.
(Post-Intelligencer Collection, Museum of History & Industry.)

On December 15, 1949, John received the following message from the architect, Marcus Priteca: "In appreciation of your client-age and your patient cooperation with our efforts, I will be pleased to have you accept our professional services in connection with the Circle and Commodore-Duchess jobs as a present to the firm."

John replied, "Your letter almost knocked me off the Christmas tree—even the tall one they have in Bellingham … Now you have really extended yourself in presenting me with a substantial and loud present. Money talks—and that is one language I understand."

This gesture from Priteca was just one of the many gifts John received every year. Gifts and gratuities flowed in from studios, film distributors, a variety of vendors, and a great many other friends and business associates. In just one season he received boxes of candy, annual calendars and personal day books, flowers, preserves, light-ers, letter openers, desk accessories, a money clip, an ash receiver, a cigarette box, playing cards, and a variety of other gadgets. He also received passes to the Seattle Rainiers baseball season, to most of the other theaters in the city, and to other local events. In turn, John and Fred sent annual passes to their counterparts in other theaters, to the studio owners, film distributors and their families, to many friends and business associates, and fortunately for us, my sisters and all our cousins. It was a great sadness to all of us in the family when the theaters were sold in the 1980s and we no longer received annual movie passes.

John proved that he could change with the times when it came to showing movies. He decided to abandon the newsreel format of Seattle Telenews. The theater had not been producing a profit from showing only newsreels. The Telenews closed on December 18, 1949. It reopened the next evening as the Capitol Theatre, showing regular features for an admission price of twenty-five cents. At the same time, the downtown Roosevelt Theatre at Fifth and Pike started showing the finer foreign films when they were available from distributors.

Capitol Theatre, ca. 1938.
(UW Special Collections, negative no. UW9109.)

Towards the end of 1949, the Uptown Theatre was about to reopen after a four-month remodel. The type of films it would show changed from foreign films to first-run domestic features. Zollie set up the Uptown at the foot of Queen Anne Hill to run "day and date" with the Palomar. This meant that first-run films booked for the Palomar downtown would also be shown at the Uptown. Zollie stated that this policy would extend the company's reach into a new district by offering Uptown patrons first-run attractions. He went on to say that the policy had many advantages. The Uptown would be a first-class house, and patrons who didn't like to come downtown because of parking problems could visit a neighborhood theater. The change would not affect the Palomar grosses.

Fred was involved in every area of the company. He wrote his friend Irv Robbins in December 1949 that the company had three drive-in theaters under construction. Fred and Irv had been friends since childhood, and Irv frequently wrote to Fred, keeping him apprised of his progress in putting together a retail ice cream company in Los Angeles with his brother-in-law, Butch Baskin. Irv had asked Fred to fill him in about popcorn sales and to advise him about the idea of selling popcorn on the street outside of the store. Sam Walton had set up a popcorn machine outside his variety store in Newport, Arkansas, and found his traffic increased. Popcorn sales at the concession stands was an area in which Fred had a great deal of expertise.

Fred wrote to Irv that a new popcorn machine could be purchased for about $700, that the markup on popcorn was tremendous with the only caveat being the expense of the labor to operate the machine and sell the popcorn. The finest South American jumbo popcorn would cost about $9.00 per hundredweight, the best seasoning was pure coconut oil with artificial coloring added, and any moron could learn to operate a popcorn machine profitably with an hour's training. He went on to say that while Sterling had found it impossible to sell popcorn on the street, the ten-cent stores seemed to do fine with machines on the street, and he referred him to another friend who sold many popcorn machines to the ten-cent stores in Southern California. Butch Baskin and Irv Robbins stuck to ice cream, apparently with some success.

At the end of the decade, the operators, also known as projectionists, earned $1.48 an hour, and an usher made $.76 an hour during the day and $1.12 at night. A cashier earned about $.69 and janitors got $1.30.

On a trip to California, Zollie met a man who owned a vacant building and had put in bowling lanes. It proved to be a successful venture, and Zollie reported this to John. John decided to try to operate bowling centers, a major shift in business.

In many ways, bowling centers were like movie houses. Instead of a screen, there were lanes. People came in, and instead of buying tickets, they rented lanes, shoes, and balls. They bought refreshments, stayed a few hours, and left. John didn't have to deal with movie distributors or rent their movies. He offered a wholesome, clean place for people to spend their time and have fun economically.

There was another advantage. Movies ran in a theater for a week so a patron could not be expected to visit more than once during a run (of course, real fans kept coming back to their favorite pictures). Bowlers might return several times a week and even play several games a night. John told Zollie to try a bowling center in the theater on Queen Anne, which wasn't doing well. The Queen Anne Theatre closed on December 31, 1949, and, after a major makeover, became the Queen Anne Bowl (the building was demolished in 2004, and a five-unit condominium and retail complex was built on the site). Sterling Theatres was recreation too.

John lived out his humanist beliefs and contributed to many causes. His charitable gifts in 1949 included $150 apiece to the National Jewish Hospital in Denver and Will Rogers Memorial Hospital in New York, $250 to the building campaign for the Museum of History and Industry, contributions to both the Times and P-I funds for the newsboys' annual Christmas dinner, the Sephardic Bikur Holim Carnival, and the Community Chest. This is just a small portion of the numerous contributions John made. He was repeatedly solicited by the Jewish Federation, Community Chest, Boys Clubs, and dozens of other organizations.

John was also active in community life. He was one of the early members of the Seattle Historical Society and a contributor to the Museum of History and Industry (MOHAI) building in 1947. He was involved in the creation of the Northwest Film Club and the Anti-Defamation League. He contributed to the Anti-TB League of King County, the American Ethical Union, the National Council of Jewish Women, American Legion, the annual Fourth of July Celebration, and the Blood Bank.

While John did not get involved in politics, except when an issue directly affected his business, he engaged with the business community through a variety of organizations. He was a member and participant of the Motion Picture Theatre Owners Association, the Independent Order of Odd Fellows, the Mutual Business Club, the Seattle Chamber of Commerce, the Ark Lodge, and the Masons. As he got older and found he had less time and energy, he resigned from the organizations in which he could no longer remain active. His activities in support of the Humanist Society increased, and in 1946 and 1947, he contributed a total of $25,000 to the humanist movement.

As early as 1942, John and Jessie established charitable trusts, which held and operated various assets and through which funds were provided to Children's Orthopedic Hospital, Children's Home Society of Washington, the Psychiatric Clinic for Children in Los Angeles, and the University of Washington. Later Jessie would also designate significant bequests to several other organizations, including the Caroline Kline Galland Home for the Aged, Jewish Family and Child Service, the Jewish Federation of Seattle, the Los Angeles Music and Art School, and the Jewish Community Center of Seattle.

John and Jessie also had active social and cultural lives. They were members of the Glendale Country Club, of which John was president in 1945, and the Washington Athletic Club. Jessie supported the Junior Symphony Orchestra and enjoyed attending the opera for many years.

With the arrival of Fred's last two children, Alison in 1948 and Rian in 1951, John and Jessie had nine grandchildren. John was in his late sixties when he wrote to a friend and business associate that, if his friend recalled the number of grandchildren he had a few years ago, he would realize that John was making progress "at least in one direction. However," John continued, "I am still not up to par as there is a preponderance of girls." He wrote to another friend who had wished him a happy birthday, "As for my formula for keeping young, it is a strenuous effort on my part to stay on this earth as long as I can, because you can easily imagine what the old boy up above will do to me when I croak."

In the five years after the end of World War II, John had taken the Sterling Theatres to a new level, and he was just getting started (see Appendix A).

Bridges to the Future

❧ 1950s ❧

In 1949, John and Fred took a trip to the east side of Lake Washington where they already operated the Bel-Vue Theatre. They were looking for property on which to build a drive-in. The idea of a drive-in theater where patrons could view movies from the comfort of their automobiles originated with New Jersey inventor Richard Hollingshead, Jr., who patented the idea. He advertised, "The whole family is welcome, regardless of how noisy the children are." In the early years, the soundtrack was broadcast across the parking lot from loudspeakers. The development of in-car speakers just before World War II solved problems of noise pollution and sound delays for viewers at the back of the lot. Bill Forman had already demonstrated that drive-ins would work in the Tacoma area, and John and Bill had partnered in the Duwamish Drive-In south of Boeing Field.

John and Fred drove over the floating bridge into the area that is now just north of Interstate 90. At the time, this was Highway 10, the Sunset Highway, which went from Seattle to eastern Washington via Snoqualmie Pass. As they explored, they saw a man working along the side of the road. They asked him if he knew of any property for sale in the area. He directed them to some land just south of the highway where they did indeed find acreage for sale. At the end of 1949, the Oak Theatre Company received approval from the King

County Planning Commission for a rezone on the Sunset Highway for the new drive-in theater, thus launching a new era in the history of Sterling Theatres.

Sunset Drive-In aerial view on Sunset Highway, Factoria, 1950.

The Sunset Drive-In opened in Factoria in September of 1950. Factoria was timberland as late as the 1920s and had been planned as an industrial center. Factoria sat in unincorporated King County and would not become part of Bellevue until 1993. As soon as it opened, the Sunset, with room for 681 cars, enjoyed immense popularity, which continued throughout the fifties and sixties. Families, high school and college students, and of course, young couples who practiced the art of fogging up the windows, all found something to enjoy at the Sunset. The drive-ins tapped a market of movie fans who found the informality and comfort of their own cars preferable to a theater seat. The focus for drive-ins was families. There were play areas where children could entertain themselves before the film started and during the "refreshment" intermission. The refreshment center was located in the Center

House, which housed the projection booth and which provided easy access from the entire theater site. This was also where the restroom facilities were located. The Center House was easy to find for young movie fans, but navigating back to the family car in a large parking lot sometimes proved a little more troublesome.

The Dalles Drive-In center house.

Drive-ins added a new dimension to the theater company. First, of course, it was another way to sell movie tickets and refreshments. But the drive-ins proved to be an excellent way to hold land until the surrounding area filled in sufficiently to support an indoor theater or some other development. John and Fred established several measures for evaluating a land purchase, including that the land be in an area they believed would grow into a strong residential community and that it be near a major highway intersection or, later, have easy access to freeway interchanges.

Bowling centers became a separate division of Sterling by 1950. The Queen Anne Theatre reopened as an eighteen-lane bowling center in November of 1950. While Bill Danz was not usually involved in operations, in this instance he was charged with supervising the amenities in the lobby, the restrooms, and the locker rooms. At that time, bowling centers had locker rooms where people could change their clothes from their work attire to more casual clothing and change into their bowling shoes.

Fred Danz, Bowl Manager Frank Cole, John Danz, Bill Danz.

Zollie Volchok became general manager of the theaters in 1950 and sat in on a conversation about the completion of the bowl with John and Bill. Part of the discussion centered on the placement of the shoehorns in the locker rooms. As always, John continued to pay close attention to even the smallest details in his businesses.

Bill had placed the shoehorns at approximately hip level, a level that would be at about shoulder height when a person was sitting to put on his or her shoes. John said something like, "Why did you put the shoe horn up there? You have to put it down here, don't you?" and he started hitting Bill's knee. "Then why did you put it so high?" He went on and on, hitting Bill on the knee.

Zollie said, "I remember like it was yesterday because it was so stupid. John Danz said the shoehorn should go down here ... and he hit his knee ... just pounded his knee."

Zollie always thought that John treated Bill very harshly, much differently than Fred, of whom John seemed more accepting. To be sure, Bill and Fred had differing personalities, but who can say what goes on between a father and his sons? Bill later said that his father was a harsh boss, too harsh. Zollie said, "He always favored Fred over Bill. It bothered me, but that's how it was. Bill never discussed it with me."

These unpleasant incidents were common, said Zollie. John might say something like, "What did the Palomar gross this week?" Bill would answer that they didn't have that information yet. Then John would yell, "You should have it ready!"

Zollie said, "[Bill] was right, but the old man didn't think so."

Bill had a difficult relationship with his father; John could not accept Bill for who he was. For example, John, as one of the prime supporters of the humanist movement in the Pacific Northwest, was convinced that religion was a negative influence on people's lives. John spoke to both of his sons about participating in the movement, about supporting the movement, and about refraining from sending their children to any religious Sunday school. Fred agreed with John, or at least seemed to. Bill, on the other hand, told John that he and his wife, Selma, had discussed it, and they were not interested. What was John's response? "Your wife should not be making decisions!" In the end, Bill's children went to Sunday school and were raised with a Jewish identity. Fred's children were aware of their Jewish heritage but were raised with an association to the Unitarian Church.

It may seem disingenuous of John when we recall that Jessie and John had been married by Rabbi Samuel Koch of Temple de Hirsch back in 1911. John's children had attended Sunday school at the temple, mainly because Jessie wanted them to. Bill would much later recall only that he attended, but he didn't think he thought anything at all about it. He recalled participating in Passover with the extended family, including grandparents, aunts, uncles, and cousins. Bill identifies as a Jew but does not have any religious beliefs. But people's opinions and philosophies change.

John's high expectations of his executives were sometimes extraordinary. He believed that his men should devote all of their free time to the business. While he encouraged his sons to pursue activities that could be of benefit to the company, he discouraged other activities. For example, John was a member of Glendale Country Club, and he encouraged his sons to join Glendale and to learn to play golf. Many a deal could be made and important relationships cultivated on the golf course and over the bridge table at the club.

Bill took his father's advice. He enjoyed both golf and bridge and was a member of Glendale from 1945 until the time of this writing, at which time he is ninety-six years old. He doesn't play golf any longer but still enjoys weekly bridge games and lunch with his cronies and often comes home the day's winner. He does a great job keeping track of the cards and playing the hands.

Fred played golf for a few years but really had little interest in the game. He loved being on the water and enjoyed sailing and the camaraderie of other sailing men and their families throughout his life.

Bill was a very good writer and enjoyed the avocation greatly. John complained that the writing did nothing to further the business and, therefore, was a waste of time. Bill refused to abide by John's demand that he stop writing short stories, poems, and other fiction in his free time, and the issue generated even more friction.

On September 28, 1951, the Northgate Theatre opened in the Northgate Shopping Center in the north end of Seattle. Northgate was the first regional shopping center in the United States to be called a mall, and the Northgate Theatre was the first to be located in one of these new developments.

The opening of the Northgate was the last major event that Bill participated in as an executive of Sterling Theatres. When I asked him what his breaking point was, he told me that his father wanted him to do something or say something to a man that he, Bill, didn't even know. Bill couldn't remember what it was or to whom he was supposed to say it, but he did recall that it would have been a very insulting thing to say, and Bill refused. We children knew nothing about the disagreement at the time. What we did know was that

Northgate Theatre
(Insert) Detail of Northgate decor

Northgate
Theatre staff
in themed
uniforms, 1951.

Crowd waiting
for Matinee
at Northgate
Theatre, 1952.

one morning we woke up and Daddy was not home. He was in the hospital with bleeding ulcers.

On March 21, 1952, Bill Danz resigned from Sterling Theatres.

About a year later, Bill's marriage to Selma ended. Bill moved into the house on Lake Washington where he lives to this day. He continued to be cordial to his father and maintained a warm, loving relationship with his mother.

⚜

Like the theaters, the bowling centers received their share of scrutiny. By this time, there were too many theaters and bowling centers for Fred and Zollie to visit them all, so John assigned additional executives to the nightly inspections of the various properties. After one visit to the Queen Anne Bowl in August of 1954, the report included both compliments to the staff on getting the alleys in shape for the new season as well as suggestions for improving other elements. The scorekeepers' tables were in bad shape and needed to be painted. Springs in the theater-type seats were sagging, a handrail was needed for the ladies' locker room, a latch was missing on the store room, and the black glass on the cash register was broken. Finally the report mentioned that the "Rental Shoes—10¢" sign would be ready the first of the following week, and while the restaurant looked neat and clean, business was very slow.

Dallas Walderon, company treasurer, visited the Queen Anne Bowl in May of 1956, apparently on a social occasion with family or friends. He noticed several problems. The shoes they rented were in poor condition, the men's room was not clean, and the ladies' room was in only fair condition. Three of the seats in the restaurant were torn, and the young waitress served ice cream sodas but forgot to put the ice cream in. He did, however, compliment the manager on the way she handled the bowling tournament that was in progress that evening.

Dallas Walderon, SRO treasurer.

Occasionally, unruly young people caused disturbances. One such incident occurred at the Northgate Theatre during the children's matinee. A boy who was acting as monitor was struck by another boy whom he was attempting to quiet down and suffered a broken nose. The matter was reported to the insurance company.

The theaters in other parts of the region were also visited regularly. After one visit to the theaters in The Dalles, Fred sent a long list of issues that needed correction with the expectation that there would be changes made, or at least in process, within a few days: an area needed cleaning, a piece of machinery did not function properly, personnel were not paying attention, and an usherette was chewing gum. In the letter, Fred noted that the gardens in the Civic Theatre needed replanting and the doorman should wear a coat and have clean hands. Every detail at every property was carefully scrutinized.

However carefully they paid attention to these details, there were some circumstances that remained beyond the control of even the most exacting administrative oversight. In January of 1950, a huge blizzard hit the Seattle area, and the city's streets were empty of traffic for several days. More than twenty inches of snow fell, and temperatures plummeted to record lows for at least eighteen days in January. The city was almost at a standstill for about three weeks.

❧ ❧

In December 1952, Sterling Theatres made a contribution of $1,400 to the Humanist Society of Washington. This was in support of the purchase of the old Labor Temple building at 600 University Street that became the headquarters for the society. John remained the prime mover and major supporter of the Humanist Society of Washington for many years. He became a long-time friend of both Professor Giovanni Costigan of the University of Washington and Rabbi Raphael Levine, the senior rabbi at Temple de Hirsh. They enjoyed great intellectual and always respectful discussions about the value, or lack, of religion in people's lives. In 1965, Professor Costigan wrote to Jessie on the occasion of a speech he gave to 175 people at the UW student humanist group in which he had paid a special tribute to John's memory. Unfortunately, Dr. Costigan did not tell Jessie what he said and only remarked that he was sorry the event had not appeared in the newspaper as no reporters were present at the meeting.

A major challenge for Seattle theater operators occurred in 1954 when Seattle created the Board of Theater Supervisors, a censorship body consisting of fifteen members. John told a friend in a letter that he thought the local theater operators did a fine job of controlling access to films by young people, and that the Board of Supervisors was an unnecessary extra layer of interference.

In early 1955, Fred asked Treasurer Dallas Walderon to research the possibility of acquiring health insurance for the sixty-seven office employees, theater managers, assistant managers, and night managers.

The plan he recommended included basic health coverage plus coverage for polio with a maximum of $5,000 and a major medical coverage with a deductible of $100 and coverage of 75 percent after the deductible to a maximum of $5,000.

Dallas recommended that the company pay the $6.25 premium for the employees and half of the $10.84 dependent's premium. The cost to the company to cover the sixty-seven employees would be an annual premium of $4,187.50, and if half the employees covered their dependents, the company's share would be $1,788.60. The total annual premium would be $5,976.10.

Another long-running company "benefit" was an annual picnic, usually held in August, to which all employees and their families were invited (some employees regarded the rain-or-shine event as an obligation). For several years, it was held at the house on Lake Washington in Madison Park. As the company grew bigger, the picnics moved to other lakefront parks in the area. The children enjoyed a variety of games and activities. The adults played too, although John thought there should be more games provided for the grownups. There was always plenty of good food and drinks, as well as prizes for the contest winners. On occasion, someone brought a boat and took people water skiing or for rides around the lake. Some years there was even a fair amount of sun.

Three legged race at the annual company picnic with jackets worn in August.

Picnic fun at Lake Sammamish.

Beginning in 1955, Fred and Zollie lent their leadership to the local unit of the Variety Club, a community service organization made up of men from entertainment and the media. Each community was a "tent," and the head was the "Chief Barker." The Variety Club was both social and service oriented, and the members enjoyed one another's company as much as the benefits they offered. The Seattle tent focused its efforts on helping children by supporting the work of Children's Orthopedic Hospital, then quickly moving from simply helping crippled youngsters to all manner of pediatric medical care.

The flamboyant members embraced the work of the hospital, but their style sometimes ran against the grain of the hospital trustees, all women and all members of established Seattle families. In 1968, Zollie approached the head of KIRO-TV with an idea for a telethon modeled after Jerry Lewis's muscular dystrophy campaigns. The telethon featured entertainment and pleas for donations around the clock. Volunteers staffed telephones to take pledges, and supporters could get on live television by delivering donations they collected.

The idea of a telethon was slow to inspire the hospital trustees, but that first year they collected $90.000, about half what the hospital's month-long Penny Drive generated. By year three, ten telephones had grown to thirty, and the Variety Club Telethon had become part of Seattle's popular culture. By 1984, twenty-two charities shared in the Variety Club's efforts.

Inauguration of the first Crew of Tent 46. Left to Right Back Row: B.C. Johnson, Doug Forbes, Paul McElheny, Harry Plunkett, Ed Cruea, C.B. Guftason, Fred Danz. Front Row: M. W. "Bud" Saffle, Jr., Frank Cristie, Art Greenfield, Al Grubstick (International Officer who came to perform the ceremony.)

Changes in the entertainment industry left the Variety Club without younger members to take the reins from Fred and Zollie's generation. In 1992, the Variety Club folded its tent.

During this time, the company started acquiring parcels of land along Highway 99 near Sea-Tac Airport in the city of Tukwila. They used the Progressive Company as the purchasing entity and eventually put together six parcels. On this land, they built a particularly wonderful hardtop theater called the Lewis & Clark, which opened on November 20, 1956. (The first film to be shown was *War and Peace*.) The theme of the theater was manifested in several ways. There was a replica of the keelboat that the Corps of Discovery rowed and hauled by hand up the Missouri River displayed in the lobby. The auditorium featured murals filling the side walls arranged by decorator Anthony B. Heinsbergen, depicting Meriwether Lewis and William Clark with Native Americans. In October of the following year, a thirty-two-lane bowling center was completed next door, connected to the theater by a breezeway. Along the back wall of the bowling center, spanning all thirty-two lanes, was a magnificent mural of the expedition created by Native American artist Del McBride (1928-1998), founder of the Klee Wyk Studio in Nisqually, Washington. The mural was designed by Del and painted directly on the wall by his brother Bud and Richard Schneider.

Keel boat.

Lewis & Clark Theatre and Bowl, 15820 Pacific Highway South, Tukwila, 1956.

Over the next fifty years, thirteen other parcels were added. Some of those parcels were acquired for as little as twenty cents per square foot. More than forty years later, in 2002, the property at the back of the theater and bowl became a large airport parking facility called Shuttle Park 2. John and Fred's penchant for acquiring property in areas likely to see significant growth paid off many times over. In December 2005, a final piece brought the total property owned to twenty-six acres.

Mural at Lewis & Clark.

Naturally, none of this expansion came without the need for capital and funding was always a challenge. When John purchased the Cheriton Fruit Gardens property in "downtown" Bellevue in

November 1955 for $350,000, he employed a strategy that continues to this day. He purchased more land than he thought he would need. The company then subdivided the property and sold off pieces, sometimes many years later, to finance the construction of new theaters.

Bellevue started as a post office in 1886 in what is today Medina. The principal industry there for many decades was the harvest of dense stands of timber. Logging operations and mills sprang up and then dissolved or moved as the crosscut saws felled the immense trees. The loggers left behind "stump ranches," barely suitable for cultivation. Hardworking farmers, notably many Japanese immigrants, cleared out the slash, and Bellevue became known for its strawberries. In 1925, residents held the first Strawberry Festival that attracted visitors from nearby Kirkland and Redmond. In 1935, fifteen thousand people attended the festival; three times the number of persons living in the area. The fifty-five Japanese American families who had farmed most of the berries were interned by the U.S. government in 1942, and their 472 acres of land passed out of their hands. By 1945, when a few of these families returned, most of the land was being laid out for residential development.

The construction of the first Lake Washington floating bridge in 1940 opened the door to large-scale development, and the area continued to grow. Efforts to incorporate Bellevue finally met with success in March 1953 with a vote by the residents of 885 to 461. Bellevue became a city.

When downtown Bellevue was designed, the blocks were laid out as double, or super blocks. John purchased property spanning from what is now the corner of 108th Avenue Northeast and Northeast Eighth Street to the pedestrian corridor on Northeast Sixth Street and on to what would have been 105th Avenue Northeast. John traded his interest in this property and the $5,000 he actually paid as earnest money in partial payment of $55,000 worth of stock in Sterling Theatre Company. Today this Bellevue property is one of the most important parcels in the corporate portfolio. As of 2010, it also remains one of the most significant pieces of under-developed property in downtown Bellevue.

The first building to be built on this property was the sixteen-lane Belle Lanes Bowl, which opened in November 1957. The bowling center was so successful that ten months later John added another sixteen lanes. The bowl featured an excellent grill and four pinball machines. The Belle Lanes Grill became a popular lunch stop for Bellevue business people.

Belle Lanes Bowl.
(Image courtesy of Eastside Heritage Center, L90-26-14.)

At the end of 1956, John completed a transaction that he had begun decades before. The company had been leasing the Colonial Theatre on Fourth Avenue near Pike in Seattle since 1917. On November 8, 1956, John purchased the Colonial property for $425,000. The company continued to operate the theater until 1972, more than fifty years of movies and vaudeville. The building was sold soon after the theater closed, and now a Starbucks is in that location.

In 1958, John began seeing a doctor about a heart ailment. He was often not well during the next couple of years but continued to go to the office whenever possible. With Bill Danz out of the business, Fred began taking the reins from his father.

᪥ ᪥

John's businesses in California, managed by Matt Appelman, continued to grow and prosper. Frequent correspondence between John and Matt continued even after Fred took on the majority of John's management duties for the California operations. In 1960, Matt sent $20,000 to

John with a letter detailing some of the activity in his organization. He wanted Fred to know how some of the pictures had done in Los Angeles (*Fugitive Kind* died, *Huckleberry Finn* was very, very strong, and *Hercules Unchained* was just fair). Matt continued his efforts to add additional land to the La Mirada Drive-In property. He also asked for a raise as he had not had an increase for seven years. John responded the next day, giving him an increase of $25 a week, about sixteen percent.

In one of his notes to Matt, John expressed concern about the competition from television and added a comment that "staring us in the face is pay T-V." He also expressed concern that "we haven't got the facilities or experience to build theatres as well as our competitors, especially at the present high prices," so he was abandoning plans to build at Costa Mesa.

A listing of Sterling Theatres Co. and Sterling Bowling Co., dated July 7, 1960, shows fourteen theaters (including the Sunset Drive-In) and three bowling centers. Ray Coach was the manager of the Admiral Theatre, Bob Bond was the assistant manager of the Colonial, Jean Chester was manager at the Magnolia, and Ib Johansen was assistant manager at the Northgate.

Ray Coach started working for Sterling in 1941 and continued for thirty years, retiring in 1971. Ray was the theater manager credited with initiating community giveaway programs in neighborhood theaters.

Bob Bond stayed with Sterling until the theaters were sold in 1986, at which time he was the operations manager.

Bob Bond,
Operations Manager

Jean Chester retired in 1971 after more than twenty-five years with the company. She said that one of her biggest thrills was helping to open the brand new John Danz Theater and becoming its manager in 1961. At the time of her retirement, she was the manager of the Bel-Vue Theatre, where she took her final curtain call.

Ib Johansen was still with the theaters when they were sold, ending his career as the impressive and well-known manager of the John Danz Theatre.

Theater managers met with administration on a regular basis. Theaters were divided into two divisions; downtown and suburban. Managers usually met separately with fifteen to twenty people, including administrative staff. One of the frequent topics at the suburban managers' meeting was the problems caused by young people on Friday nights. The report from the meeting at the end of August 1960 states that "the first two Friday nights in September can make or break the theatre manager's business" so they needed to be prepared to meet the onslaught by showing them "who is the boss." Recommendations included constant patrol of the theater aisles (with a "one warning and you're out" policy) and reminders about the theater standards in an on-screen trailer. Managers were encouraged to train the ushers well, to let the kids know the theaters' standards, enforce those standards, and not back down.

Other items of discussion included deodorant blocks in rest rooms, "exploitation ideas" (advertising and promotion), "sorry passes" to be used for full houses, and the current theater competitions.

The downtown managers didn't have the same Friday night problems. Their discussions included issues with cashiers, former employees trying to gain free access, the prizes for current competitions, and smoking in theater lobbies. But they, too, struggled with deodorant blocks in the rest rooms.

Both groups discussed a variety of reporting and communication issues.

❧ ❧

John and Jessie Danz on the occasion of their fiftieth wedding anniversary.

March 19, 1961 brought nineteen members of the Danz family together in Seattle to celebrate Jessie and John's fiftieth wedding anniversary.

In October 1961, John and Jessie made a gift valued at more than $330,000 to the University of Washington. The John Danz Fund (called the Jessie and John Danz Fund after Jessie's death) was established to bring scholars of international reputation to the campus, specifically "persons who have concerned themselves with the impact of science and philosophy on man's perception of a rational universe." Lectures were intended to include part of the humanist philosophy, but for many years that piece has been left out of the literature and the lecture introductions. Giovanni Costigan wrote to Jessie, "out of regard for your husband's strong convictions this omission should be remedied." It never was. As of 2010, the Danz Fund is operated by the university's Graduate School and still brings many remarkable speakers to campus for presentations to the community.

John's failing health forced him to spend more time at home on the top floor of the Narada. He enjoyed watching the transformation of the foot of Queen Anne Hill into the site of the Century 21 Exposition—the Seattle World's Fair.

View of Seattle Center from John's window.

John Danz, born Israel Danowsky, died of heart disease on October 25, 1961, the day before the gift to the University of Washington was announced. Public recognition of his accomplishments and remembrances and floral tributes flooded in. His many business associates naturally offered their condolences to the family, but there was another, perhaps more touching tribute. Thousands of young people had worked for John in the theaters and bowling centers during the previous fifty years. Many acknowledged the lessons they had learned under his demanding tutelage as formative in their future successes.

John Danz is representative of a tradition of immigrant entre-preneurs. He rode a peddler's wagon to the top of a theater and real estate empire. He was able to transition from house wares to clothing to nickelodeons to full-scale movie houses and bowling centers, always focused on real estate investment, using little formal education, an abundance of intelligence, a penchant for secrecy, a balance of risk taking and caution, and an intense ambition to make a good deal. Just as he was not afraid to jump from shirts and trousers to motion pictures, he was willing to take the leap from the movies to bowling centers. Every doorman, usher, and usherette represented him person-ally, and he made that clear to each of them. His drive came at some cost as evidenced by the strained relationships with his eldest son and his brother. John never forgot the community that helped him prosper. He gave back where he could, notably to programs benefitting youth. In this manner, he was very Jewish by culture, if not by religion. In the Jewish tradition, children are taught early and often the obligation of *tzedakah*. The term is usually translated as "charity" in modern times, but the origin comes from the word "justice" and the idea that all belongs to G-d,[3] all is distributed in ways we are not able to understand, and it is our duty to distribute what we are fortunate to have to those less fortunate. Righteous giving and just behavior ensures the basic well-being of our fellow human beings

John's grandchildren don't seem to have many memories of interacting directly with him. We remember going to his apartment for Thanksgiving dinner every year and recall that he gave each of us as many silver dollars as years we were old (I wish I had put them in a safe deposit box!). Every year he would ask each of us to stand next to him and say what we were thankful for. Some of the cousins recall being afraid of and intimidated by him and don't remember him as the kind of grandpa on whose lap you felt warm and comfortable (although old home movies show him being affectionate with us children).

I had one particular experience with John that was unforgettable. I must have been ten or twelve years old and was downtown with my best friend, Lynne. We were waiting to go home with my dad and wanted to watch the movie while we waited. I think we were told specifically not to go in the balcony, but I told Lynne it was okay, even though the balcony was closed. When we were discovered by a very stern John Danz, I was punished by losing my precious theater pass for an entire year. I learned my lesson the hard way.

Jessie was warm, caring, patient, and non-judgmental. She would occasionally take one or two of her granddaughters to the Bon Marché for lunch in the Tea Room. We would sometimes spend the night with Jessie and John, usually Barbara and JoAnne together, Penny and Laurie together, and I think Tad and I spent time together there a couple of times. Sometimes one or both of my sisters and I would

---

3   Many Jews write the word G-d so that the name of the Lord cannot be destroyed or discarded disrespectfully.

spend the night. Alison also recalls sharing many special moments with Jessie.

Michael Forman, Dorothy's son and John's eldest grandson, recalls that as he walked past their building every morning on the way to school, they would be having breakfast by the window or on their little balcony and would wave and call to him. He also remembers the time when he and a friend flew a great many paper airplanes off the balcony and that they landed in the neighbors' yards. Both the neighbors and Jessie and John were upset with Mike.

The Next Generation

❧ 1961–1977 ❧

John's will established a trust, creating a family dynamic that played out for more than thirty years. It also revealed his somewhat chauvinistic attitudes. He left his share of the company and personal assets in trust to seven of his nine grandchildren. Dorothy's children did not benefit much in John's will, nor later in Jessie's. Her will says, specifically, "I have not made any substantial provision [for my daughter] for the reason that her financial situation is greatly superior [to that of the other children and grandchildren]. John did leave a token bequest of money to both Michael and JoAnne Forman, some shares in Sterling Theatres Co. to Bill, life gifts to Jessie and his sister Lillie, and ten percent of his interest in the California properties to Matt Appelman. All of his personal effects he left to Jessie. The rest of the trust income was divided, with half returning to the trust and the other half going to Fred, who was also the trustee of both John and Jessie's trusts.

At the time of his death, John and Jessie's personal estate included the Admiral Theatre, the Beacon Theatre, the Columbia Building in Longview, the Narada Apartment Building, the Granada Theatre, the Roosevelt Theatre, and various shares of stock in publicly traded companies. The estate also included shares in nine different companies comprising the Sterling organization.

John ensured that Fred's two boys, Tad and Rian, would have a controlling interest by leaving each of them three shares of his trust while each of the five girls—Barbara, Carolee, Penny, Laurie, and Alison—received one share each. Six shares to five. Rian was ten years old when John died. Tad was nineteen. It seems to me that John must have assumed that these boys would grow into strong, sharp, competent men who would not only want to operate the company as he did but would also be capable of doing so. I think he also assumed that the girls would marry and that their husbands would take care of them; they might run a household, or maybe teach or be secretaries. That the girls would enter the business did not seem to be a possibility for him. John and, later, Jessie also gave Fred, as trustee, discretion to help with education, housing and medical needs for the grandchildren who were the ultimate beneficiaries of the trusts.

The will gave Fred full control of the company for the duration of his lifetime, but the trusts would not be distributed until the death of the last of John's children.

Jessie was elected to a seat on the board of each of the many companies and remained an active participant in the businesses until her death in 1973. Fred was elected president of all the companies and continued to run the entire organization for the next thirty-eight years. In her will, Jessie changed the balance of control somewhat by leaving her half of the company in equal shares to the seven children of Fred and Bill and an income for life to Bill.

Shortly after his marriage ended in 1953, Bill began dating long-time friend Carolyn Blumenthal Taylor, and they were married on December 10, 1959. John and Jessie were extremely pleased with this union. As a wedding gift, they gave Bill and Carolyn the house and property on Lake Washington. About six years later, Jessie loaned Carolyn the money for construction of a new house on the property. To keep it equitable, Jessie left Fred the Admiral Theatre.

The winter after Bill and Carolyn moved into their new house, Jessie came down with the flu. Carolyn went to Jessie's Queen Anne apartment and brought her back to the house to care for her. When she recovered, Jessie returned home, but the next day she phoned to say she missed Bill and Carolyn and wanted to come live with them. Carolyn was pleased to say yes, and Jessie lived happily with them for six years until her death in 1973.

❦ ❦

The early 1960s brought great change to the character of Seattle and the Puget Sound Region. The most obvious development came in the mid fifties as community and business leaders from the Seattle Chamber of Commerce looked for a way both to commemorate the Alaska-Yukon-Pacific Exposition of 1909 and to showcase the city's and the region's accomplishments as the original exposition had. The state legislature formed a commission for a second World's Fair, but time constraints bumped the target date from 1959 to 1962.

Planners focused on twenty-eight acres already mostly owned by the City of Seattle at the foot of Queen Anne Hill. The Century 21 Exposition, better known as the Seattle World's Fair, took shape. The iconic Space Needle with its revolving restaurant rose 605 feet in the air and became the symbol of Seattle. From their perch on top of Queen Anne Hill, Jessie and John had a great view of the process.

The fair ran all during the summer of 1962 and attracted ten million visitors. The exposition's themes showcased the promise of science and the technology of tomorrow. At the close, Seattle received from the fair commission the land and buildings, which became the Seattle Center. The visitors left with a new image of the city, which was only a little more than a hundred years old.

The fair also left the leaders of the region with a serious can-do attitude. In the 1950s, Jim Ellis had proposed and promoted Metro—the Municipality of Metropolitan Seattle—in order to clean up Lake Washington by consolidating and improving sewage treatment. Metro successfully improved the water quality of the lake and Puget Sound.

The University of Washington, under its visionary president Charles Odegaard and with the sponsorship of the state's U.S. Senators Warren Magnusson and Henry Jackson, grew dramatically from an adequate state institution to a world-class center for research and innovation. The Boeing Company built upon its designs for jet bombers and produced the Model 707 in 1953, destined to become the most successful jetliner of the era. Boeing assumed and retained its role as the world's leading designer and manufacturer of airliners. The artificial kidney, the heart defibrillator, and the fiberglass ski emerged from the minds of local engineers, scientists, and sportsmen.

A less attractive but no less important event was the construction of Interstate 5, which eventually connected the Mexican and Canadian borders with a non-stop, high-speed, limited-access highway. In Seattle alone, the right of way consumed over five thousand homes. The economic benefits of this critical artery, really an aorta, of commerce cannot be overstated. Completion of Interstate 405, which looped around Lake Washington to the east to connect Renton and Lynnwood through Bellevue, tied in those suburbs more closely with Seattle, each other, and the rest of the state.

To complement these wonders of concrete and steel, the state added a second floating bridge between Seattle and the east side where development was continually increasing. The first floating bridge soon became obsolete, and state engineers planned its twin. Commerce flourished, and real estate developers laid out new communities that would one day become cities.

Fred Danz faced huge challenges as he took over his new role at the helm of the Sterling companies. It was sometimes a struggle for Fred and his staff just to understand what John had been involved in, as he had been very secretive in his dealings and his plans. Some properties belonged to him and Jessie, and some belonged to the companies. Even as his health was failing, there was a great deal of information he shared with no one, not even Fred.

After John's death, Fred received a letter from a long-time friend of John's who had visited him in Seattle early in 1961. He wrote to Fred, "One of the highest compliments that could be said in the affections of a father for a son was made to me during several happy hours I spent with John … We had been reminiscing about a friendship covering some twenty years and, in a moment of quiet reflection, he told me, 'I have great confidence in Fred and if, in the period ahead, you have reason to enter any discussion with him, I'd like you to feel in talking with him you'll be talking with me.'" John may never have told Fred directly of the confidence he felt in him—he was not known for giving great compliments or expressing himself in that way—but through his friend, he made sure Fred knew of his true feelings.

Fred Danz.

Fred continued to follow the path laid out by John, albeit with his own vision and fresh energy. His first task was to oversee completion of the new theater in Bellevue. It had been planned with a nautical theme but had not been formally named. I was never able to learn what name had been planned for this venue, but I know that John never would have approved the naming of a theater or building after himself. The board agreed, with Jessie's approval, to name the new venue The John Danz Theatre. The John Danz opened on December 22, 1961 and became the premier motion picture house on the Eastside until it closed in 1994.

John Danz Theatre on 106th Ave Northeast, Bellevue, ca. 1969.
(Image courtesy of Eastside Heritage Center, 1998.25.33.)

Audience seated in John Danz Theatre auditorium, ready for
grand opening ceremonies.

I asked David Schooler, who joined Sterling in 1979, what Fred
was like as the president of the company. "Fearsome" he said. There
is a story about Fred going into a theater in Longview. Jerry Kivela,
the supervisor in Longview, saw him enter the darkened auditorium

while the movie was showing. Jerry took off in the other direction, but Fred saw him. Fred upbraided him fiercely saying something to the effect of, "Don't you ever run away from me!"

David said:

> People respected him and feared him. It was very much Fred's company in many ways ... in work habits, quality and standards. We were a step cleaner and better designed than our competition. Fred seemingly worked harder than anybody else; sometimes here earlier, many times here later, many times in the evening and weekends. He visited theaters even then at that stage.

David confirmed that people who worked for Fred developed tremendous loyalty to him. It seemed to his employees that the work and life standards he set for himself were even higher than those he set for them. Fred was charming, smart, honest in his dealings, and fiscally tight ... very tight. Fred was his father's son.

David continues that Fred created a great place to work. He was exceptionally smart, savvy, and curious, loyal, hard-working, and had an excellent, though parched, sense of humor. In his time and under his leadership, SRO became the largest exhibitor in the state. He bought and built theaters in Spokane, the Tri-Cities, Walla Walla, Bellingham, and then in Portland, Oregon.

Fred was also one of the founders of the Bellevue Downtown Development Board (now Bellevue Downtown Association) and served on its board for about ten years. He was also part of a small group appointed by the mayor of Bellevue that charted the future course of downtown Bellevue.

❦ ❧

In June 1961, the company closed the purchase of the Covina Drive-In in a suburb east of Los Angeles. Over the next few years, the company's California holdings expanded considerably. Fred and Matt Appelman leased land in Torrance for a new hard-top theater. They opened the

Rolling HillsTheatre in October 1963. Later that year they purchased the Upland Grove Theatre in Upland, California.

Rolling Hills Theatre.

Weeks before her death in October 2010, Matt's widow, Frances, wrote to me:

> Matt continued to run the California Sterling organization. He built several theaters including the Pasadena Hastings [on the site of the old Hastings Drive-In Theatre], La Mirada, Covina, and the Rolling Hills ... helping SRO become successful. He even liked working with John.

> Matt had no significant difficulties with either John or Fred. They were good relationships and everyone seemed to get along well through all those years. Matt began by doing everything for the theaters, but eventually hired others to book the films, supervise the staff at the theaters, etc. while he managed the growing Southern California business.

That John would trust Matt so implicitly to operate the business on his behalf so far away was a reflection of Matt's professional character, given John's strict demands on his other managers. Fred shared this trust. Matt continued to operate the division until he retired in 1978.

The Bel-Vue Theatre operated at Bellevue Square from when the shopping center first opened in 1946. In 1964, Fred was renegotiating with Bellevue Square owner Kemper Freeman regarding rents to be charged on road show films. However, as Kemper did not have a strong background in the motion picture business, Fred provided information to help Kemper determine his rates. Although I don't know exactly what Sterling was paying Bellevue Square in 1964, in the 1980s, it was probably about 10 percent of the box office for regular first-run films with deductions for unusually high film rental expenses. Fred was being squeezed by higher rates charged by the studios and distributors for big road shows. He wrote that the film rental fee for the previous year had been 24 percent of box office gross, a normal and reasonable percentage. The rate for a road show like *Cleopatra* would be 60 percent, also normal. He continued with the expectation that ticket prices would be raised from $1.00 to $1.50 and that the expected box office gross would as much as triple ordinary box office receipts. Simple math showed that both the film company and the landlord would prosper while the theater tenant (Sterling) would suffer.

Kemper responded with an offer that the rate could remain the same with Sterling reporting gross sales as usual, and then deducting costs above the normal 25 percent to arrive at a net sales figure to be used in computing the rent. Fred frequently worked with people by providing them with the information they needed in order to make reasonable decisions.

❧ ❧

During the 1960s, each of Fred's four children worked at Sterling. Tad began working in the theaters in high school. When he moved on to college at Yale, he returned in the summers to fill in when theater managers were on vacation and then after college, returned again to Seattle where he worked at Sterling for a few months.

When a family quarrel resulted in Fred firing Tad (Tad usually adds "for the first time"), Tad and his wife Barbara returned to New York where Tad earned an MBA from Columbia. He worked in

Chicago for Corning Glass Works from 1968 until he went to work for Matt Appelman in the California Sterling operation in early 1970.

Laurie and Alison each worked in theaters during high school. One night Laurie was cashiering at the John Danz in Bellevue. A patron had a complaint and was not happy with Laurie's response. He said he would complain to Fred Danz as they were friends. She said, "OK, but I'll do you one better. He's my father."

Alison worked at the John Danz and occasionally at the Bel-Vue until she graduated from high school. During college, she worked downtown at the Town Theatre ticket office, at the Music Box, and during the summer, in the main office. She worked full time in various positions, including assistant to General Manager Jerry Vitus and even as her dad's assistant in the early seventies. Alison worked in every department except payroll and advertising, continuing until she had three children to care for. She returned to the company in the summer of 1997, working part time, doing lease administration.

Rian, Fred's youngest child, worked for the company when he was in high school and college part time. After finishing school, he worked at the radio station in San Jose (KHTT-AM and KSJO-FM), as an internal auditor in Seattle, in the bowls, and in the main office as a film buyer. He was never able to settle into a role that suited both him and the company.

❦

In February 1963, the Seattle City Council required that all motion pictures that would "tend to impress those minors under 18 years of age as advocating or condoning activities beyond the customary limits of decency in the community, or would tend to incite such minors to unlawful conduct" be classified as "adults only." The council gave the City Theater Board the job of defining and categorizing obscenity, effectively preventing single eighteen- to twenty-one-year olds from attending a great many films. It was the most restrictive policy in the country. But Seattle restrictions did not apply in Bellevue or Tukwila where patrons could see the films they wanted.

Fred expanded the theater division when he purchased the leaseholds of several theaters from the Edris Company. The Music Box, the Orpheum, the Music Hall, and the Blue Mouse came into the Sterling organization. The Music Hall was built in the 1920s as the Mayflower Theatre for vaudeville and other stage productions but was not completed and never opened under that name. It became a movie house as the Roxy in the 1930s. The Roxy soon closed because, at Seventh Avenue and Olive Street, it was just too far from the main part of city. Fox Theatres bought it and renamed it the Fox, but the Depression forced Fox to close it a second time. Then in 1934, Hamrick-Evergreen (John Hamrick was a competitor of John Danz) opened it as the Music Hall. Sterling purchased the Music Hall at the end of 1964 and completed a major renovation, re-opening it in 1967 as the Seattle 7th Avenue Theatre.

Music Hall Theatre, 1957.

Music Box Theatre.
(Post-Intelligencer Collection, Museum of History & Industry.)

Orpheum Theatre.
(Post-Intelligencer Collection, Museum of History & Industry.)

Fred tried some innovative programming, bringing in an oper-
etta film series (which was then repeated as it was very popular). The
1963 series included *Naughty Marietta*, *The Student Prince*, *Maytime*,
Brigadoon, *The Firefly*, and *Bittersweet*. Attendees sent notes and
letters complimenting the company on the series, but one customer
commented that Thursday nights would be better because on Tuesday
nights there were good television shows to watch. Another program
brought back favorite films, while a third showed classic children's
movies in selected theaters.

For several years, Fred even ran some exploitation films at the
Roosevelt Theatre but couldn't make them work so they finally got
out of the business. Exploitation films were often low-budget films
that exploited sex, violence, or perhaps romance or a big name star
and usually depended on creative, sensational advertising to attract
an audience. He commented to a film distributor that, while Herold
Greenlin in Ohio seemed to be able to operate the sex and exploitation films successfully, Sterling could not.

While Seattle and the rest of the nation struggled with the social
and political turmoil of the late 1960s, other changes swept the local
scene. Much of downtown Seattle dated to the turn of the twentieth
century and reconstruction after the Great Fire of 1889. With a few
exceptions, the Central Business District had not been updated for
more than forty years. Pioneer Square and the Pike Place Market
were positively decrepit, as were many properties further uptown.
Federal and state law allowed developers to use eminent domain to
condemn property and take it over to tear it down. Planners looked
at crumbling, vacant, and rat-infested structures built at the time
of the Klondike Gold Rush and saw the potential for steel and glass
skyscrapers and handsome profits. This was urban renewal.

Among the first slums to go was the quirky Seattle Hotel at James
and Yesler Streets, once an elegant hostelry but, by 1961, simply a
slum, home only to rats and the homeless. The wrecker's ball reduced
it to rubble to make room for an equally quirky but far less appealing
parking structure popularly dubbed "the sinking ship garage."

In the mid-1950s, visionaries formed Allied Arts to promote public funding for the arts. They helped pass bond issues to upgrade the Civic Auditorium. The organization supported the World's Fair but included in its scope the preservation of historic buildings. Allied Arts member and University of Washington Professor Victor Steinbrueck led a grassroots political movement that helped establish protections for Pioneer Square (1969) and the Pike Place Market (1971) as historic districts. When the city and the state planned a freeway through the University of Washington Arboretum, citizens said "enough!" The government's "can-do" attitude bumped up against one of "is this really necessary?"

Sadly, the elegant, old Palomar was sold and demolished in May 1965 to make room for a parking structure. The company offices moved out of the Palomar to 975 John Street at the south end of Lake Union. Between the Seattle Theatre Board and organizations like Friends of the Market, Fred must have found Seattle a far less attractive place to do business than had his father and grandfather. Fortunately, on November 30, 1965, the King County Superior Court declared unconstitutional the city ordinances prohibiting obscenity in movie showings and advertisements and establishing the Board of Theater Supervisors. The case had been brought by the Sterling Theatre Chain, the Fine Arts Guild, and a group of distributors representing Hollywood studios.

❧ ❧

In the meantime, Fred changed things around in California. Matt Appelman filed corporate papers for Sterling Men's Wear to serve as a holding company for entities there just as it had in Washington. Then sometime around 1965, Texan Jay Dauley, who worked at odd jobs and as an electrician, approached Matt about renting the front of the La Mirada Drive-In for a swap meet.

Swap meets captured the flavor of ancient bazaars and the Paris Flea Market. I could not discover the exact origins of swaps at drive-in theaters, but by 1965 more than twenty operated throughout southern California. It was a perfect use for drive-ins during the day when movies could not be shown. Theater owners rented the otherwise unused lots to organizers who, in turn, rented stall space to anyone who had something to sell from used clothing and house wares to valuable antiques. The operator could even charge an admission fee to the buyers. Shoppers looking for bargains or hidden treasures flocked to the largely unregulated events for good buys or just good fun. (Another use for empty drive-in theater lots during the week has been park-and-ride lots.)

La Mirada Swap.

The La Mirada started its swap meet in 1962 and, by July of 1977, had added a mid-week operation on Wednesdays and Thursdays. Matt formed a joint venture/partnership, called Swap-o-Rama. Dauley ran the swap field, and Sterling operated the snack bar. (Matt discovered that swap meet fans consumed more food and drink than did movie fans.) Dauley, an ambitious entrepreneur, opened new meets on vacant lots in Bakersfield and Phoenix. These were not located on theater properties and operated during the week and on some evenings as well as weekends. The Phoenix Swap, which had covered spaces with electrical outlets, did its biggest business on Wednesday nights. The covered spaces were greatly coveted during the hot Arizona summers. The Bakersfield Swap would often draw as many as twelve thousand people on its busiest days.

Dauley built a chain of flea markets in San Francisco, Texas, Louisiana, Oklahoma, Florida, and Illinois. When he ran into difficulties, he added Bakersfield and Phoenix to the Swap-o-Rama partnership, and Sterling eventually bought Dauley out of all three swaps, controlling 100 percent of Swap-o-Rama. SRO sold the Bakersfield Swap-o-Rama, part of Capitol Amusement, at the end of 1986 when Capitol was dissolved.

Tad wrote that the Phoenix Swap never proved successful and SRO sold it in the early 1980s for $5 million. Jerrill Kaplan, SRO's attorney, shrewdly insisted that the buyer obtain a letter of credit from Continental Illinois Bank for the full purchase price. When the economy tanked and the buyer defaulted, SRO went to the bank to collect. The banker said that he never expected to cash the letter of credit and reluctantly paid the obligation.

❧ ☙

One of Fred's first projects as president was to create a retirement program called (and still called) the Sterling Employees' Fund for the Future to help employees secure their long-term financial security. As far as I have been able to discover, there were no benefits for employees during John's tenure, although health insurance for executives and management might have been added in the mid-fifties after Dallas Walderon's research into the topic. John operated a very old-fashioned business. Employees were paid for their work and received only some small amount of vacation and perhaps some sick leave. Most employees were paid wages on an hourly basis. Executives received a monthly salary, but they were also expected to devote much more than forty hours a week to the company's needs.

The Fund for the Future was created as a retirement program in which both the company and the employee participated. Most employees were young and worked for the company for just a few years. These were usually the ushers, cashiers, pin boys, and grill staff. Under Fund for the Future, an employee had to be twenty-five years old to participate as well as have been employed for one year, and everyone who met the qualifications was automatically enrolled. Every year or two, the program would be explained again in *The Spotlight* for the benefit of newer employees. *The Spotlight* of October 1972 gives some details:

> The employee can either contribute to the program to increase his share or he may choose not to contribute and still receive a share of the contribution the company will make in his behalf each year.

An employee earning $5,000 a year (given certain assumptions) and not contributing to the program would leave the company at the end of fifteen years with approximately $15,000. A 3-percent employee contribution in the same fifteen years would change the figure to $20,000. The thirty-year amount would be $72,000 with no employee contribution and $95,000 with the 3-percent contribution. A $95,000 nest egg against a salary of, say, $8,000 a year (assuming raises over the career) was not a bad deal.

In years when a company didn't show a profit, it did not contribute to the fund. For example, in 1966, the Globe Amusement Company, which owned the Colonial and Music Box theaters, had a loss and so did not make a contribution to the Employees Fund. But in 1967, having shown a year-end profit, Globe resumed its contributions.

For executive personnel Fred created an additional plan. The highest-level managers were eligible to enroll in the new Capitol Amusements Company. Capitol owned theaters, bowling centers and other businesses and their value as well as their income belonged to Capitol. Sterling operated Capitol's entities. When an executive retired he – almost always a he – was given the value of his percentage of the company. Every year of participation increased the executive's share.

❧ ❧

In the meantime, the company continued its pursuit of excellence in every venue. Bowling centers received regular visits from secret shoppers. Evaluations of Belle Lanes and Queen Anne Bowl in January of 1965 reported on the state of operations, including comments on exterior lighting, signage, and cleanliness; the number of personnel in attendance; the number of patrons bowling, eating, playing pool, pinball, or other games; how well the pin-setting machines functioned; and the behavior of staff, bowling participants, and spectators. The grill, food, and service were also reviewed. There was a detailed report about a sixty-three-cent purchase that was not rung up and, on a night when Belle Lanes was operating at capacity, a comment on the inability to adequately staff areas such as the merchandise room and the billiards room.

Zollie Volchok returned to SRO in 1970

Zollie Volchok had been a good friend of both Bill and Fred since John recruited him to live in Seattle in 1946. He was someone Fred always trusted and with whom he felt he could discuss the various issues with which he was wrestling. Zollie left the company in 1953 to operate Northwest Releasing, a highly successful concert-promotion and talent-booking agency. After fifteen years, he retired from Northwest Releasing. Fred asked him to come to Sterling as the president's special assistant to allow Fred to concentrate on bringing the Seattle Pilots baseball team back to Seattle (Fred had been instrumental in bringing the team to town in the first place). While Fred admitted that he didn't particularly like baseball, he thought it was important for the city to have a major league sports team. Promoters had recently acquired the Seattle Super Sonics Basketball team, and the Washington State Stadium Commission was making plans to build the Kingdome, a covered sports venue, which had yet to find any teams.

Zollie didn't want to go back to work. Northwest Releasing had been a financial success, and he wanted to enjoy what he had accomplished. But Fred convinced him that he could spend just two or three days a week on the Sterling business. In January of 1970, Zollie returned to SRO as the assistant to the president. Fred was busy working with community leaders, like Jim Ellis (at Metro) and Eddie Carlson (his doodle on a cocktail napkin became the Space Needle), as they tried to raise the money to purchase the team from the bankrupt owners. When the league pronounced Sicks' Seattle Stadium in the Rainier Valley to be inadequate, Fred and his confederates needed money and a stadium so the American League would allow the team to stay in Seattle. Had Seattle been successful, it would have been the only major league baseball team to be community-owned. Zollie agreed to help out, but first he and Sylvia were taking a trip to Israel.

Sam Shulman, owner of the Sonics reached Zollie by phone in Israel. Sam wanted Zollie to take over as manager of the Sonics. Zollie said, "I don't know anything about basketball." Sam replied, "Neither do my players." Zollie couldn't turn down the opportunity, so he agreed to work half time for the Sonics and half time for Fred.

The baseball supporters lost the Pilots to Milwaukee (Washington Attorney General Slade Gorton sued Major League Baseball for moving the Pilots and won, resulting in the debut of the Seattle Mariners in 1977). Zollie stayed with the Sonics for fifteen years before retiring for the final time. He was general manager when the team won the National Basketball Association championship in 1979. In 1983, he was honored as NBA Executive of the Year. In 1979, Zollie accepted a seat on the board of directors of SRO and for the next twenty years remained a valuable advisor to Fred and to the company.

❧ ❧

In Los Angeles, Tad Danz worked for Matt Appelman as a film buyer and supervisor in theaters and at swap meets until 1973. When Fred acquired the American Song Festival, Tad worked with that project for about ten years. During these years, he gained experience in all the Southern California units, including theaters, radio, swap meets, and bowling. Tad also got experience in all aspects of business, including negotiating a deal, working with banks, and securing loans.

Fred had an idea that he could do some significant cross promotions between radio stations and the theaters, so he set out to buy radio stations. By 1970, SRO operated four Northwest radio stations—KBFW in Bellingham, KALE in the Tri-Cities, KEDO in Longview, and KODL in The Dalles, Oregon. Then, since there was a demand for trained disc jockeys and newscasters, SRO decided to help fill the demand by joining forces with Jerden Industries, Inc. of Seattle (the Northwest's leading record manufacturer and producer of singles and albums) in opening and operating a Ron Bailie School of Broadcasting and Electronics.

He later purchased another nine radio stations in Washington, Oregon, Colorado, and California. The cross-promotion idea was not as successful as he expected, and the stations were not particularly lucrative. But radio was a business that interested Fred, and he enjoyed it. By 1978, one of his stations, KZOK, had become the number-one FM station in Seattle.

In California, the company took over operation of the sixty-lane Parkway Bowl in El Cajon, just outside of San Diego in August of 1971. The giant complex included a restaurant, coffee shop, nursery, billiards room, a whole set of banquet rooms, and a fantastic night club theater as well. SRO then acquired land in Montclair and Pasadena, California and a lot near the Cinerama theater in Seattle in a trade with Paccar for the Bellevue land on the west side of 106th Avenue Northeast, a piece of the original Bellevue Chariton Fruit Gardens property. The California office tested the idea of senior citizen matinees, an expansion on the kiddie matinees of the 1940s and 1950s. These proved to be a hit.

Parkway Bowl.

Sterling expanded in California again in May of 1977 by acquiring seven theaters from Century Cinema Circuit, Inc., bringing the total to eighteen: The Capri in West Covina, Colorado in Pasadena, Crest in Westwood, Roxy in Glendale, Paramount and Holly in Hollywood, and Carriage Square Twin in Oxnard/Ventura.

Carriage Square Twin, Oxnard/Ventura.

In Washington, an all-day, eight-band rock festival called Sunshine Sunday was held at the Sunset Drive-In in October of 1972 with five thousand people in attendance. Rock bands performing included Taxi, Onyx, Clover, Black on White Affair, Sneaky Sam's Lamb, The Back Porch Review, Cargo—a new band from Memphis, and the Wackers, a nationally known group from Canada. County requirements for a rock festival permit were extensive and demanding because of problems arising from other rock festivals, but a team of experienced theater managers pulled it together so that it developed into one of the smoothest running outdoor music festivals that had ever been held in the Northwest. Later in the evening, the film, *The Concert for Bangladesh,* was shown, and all day and evening, food and drinks were available from the snack bar. Despite all the planning, the thousands of young people in attendance created such a mess that the janitorial company that came in to clean up late that night took one look and quit on the spot.

The company finished building the Samish Drive-In in Bellingham, which featured the first (and probably still the only) drive-in radio station. KBFW's studio sat on top of the center house.

Building on the swap meet idea that was so successful in southern California, Sterling started a regular swap meet at the Puget Park Drive-In in Everett in the summer of 1972. More than three thousand buyers and sellers turned out for the first Snohomish County Swap Meet, a pretty good indication that the concept would be popular in the Northwest. The Puget Park meet continued for thirty-seven years and became a community institution. The meet closed in 2010 after a portion of the land was sold to Swedish Hospital for a new emergency center. Another swap meet was started at the River-Vue Drive-In in Tri Cities, Washington, in April of 1977.

Swap-o-Rama ticket

Buyers and sellers at Puget Park Swap Meet.

SRO renovated the Lewis & Clark single-screen theater near Sea-Tac to become a triplex in 1975—three theaters under one roof. This allowed a family with differing tastes to go to the movies together while Sterling operated a single ticket booth and concession stand. More important, it encouraged people to attend a convenient theater more than once a week. A movie fan could see a movie and view the previews for other shows playing at the same convenient place. Sometimes people attended an early movie and stayed for a later one too, catching a bite to eat at the snack bar between showings.

Another transfer from California was a young Mike Lancaster. Mike was sixteen and working at the Lancaster Drive-In Theater when he met Terry, the daughter of the theater manager. They married three years later. After his military service, he went to work for the old Fox West Coast Circuit as a theater manager. Fox moved him three times from 1970 to 1972—Eugene, Oregon, then Everett, then back to Sacramento. In the meantime, his father-in-law transferred to Seattle to manage the Coliseum for Fox. He let Mike know that Sterling had a manager's position open in Seattle so Mike and Terry headed north in March of 1973 and Mike took over the Eastside Drive-In. Mike continued to work in Sterling theaters until 1986 when he stepped in to head the Video Division. This proved timely, given the sale of the theater division later that year. Mike Lancaster is now (2011) a senior property manager for Sterling Realty Organization and is our longest serving employee at thirty-eight years and counting.

Mike Lancaster. Insert: as Superman.

Fred continued John's tradition of service to patrons. Tall, bald Ib Johansen was representative of the career employee who embraced this spirit of excellence. Ib worked for Sterling from the early 1950s until the theaters were sold in 1986. He was a Dane who fled the Nazis, worked in Switzerland as an intelligence agent for the Allies, and served as an interpreter at the Nuremberg War Crimes Trials. He made his way to Seattle via Canada, Detroit, and ballroom-dancing instruction. He managed the Neptune, the John Danz, the Northgate, and the 7th Avenue, always distinct in his black turtleneck and dark suit. Ib was asked to be the manager when Sterling opened the Grand Alderwood Cinemas, a prestigious acknowledgement of his skill and value to the company. He helped the young people under his tutelage to learn self-discipline and attention to detail. Jackie King, who started at sixteen as an usherette and moved on to bookkeeper, said of him,

"In Mr. Johansen's theaters there was no necking, no rowdiness. He wouldn't permit it."

Long-time theatre manager Ib Johansen.

In 2002, *Seattle Times* film critic John Hartl recalled of Sterling and the Northgate, "Seattle's top theater chain. Immaculate. Cleaned after every showing. You could eat off that floor."

Always interested in new ventures, Fred spent a great amount of his time in late 1970 and early 1971 working on televising the Muhammad Ali-Joe Frasier boxing match. SRO and Tom Hullet of Concerts West had purchased the rights to the March 8, 1971 fight for Northern California, Oregon, Washington, Texas, Utah, Colorado, Nevada, and Western Canada. Zollie Volchok worked on the project as a representative of SRO. Fred reported later that "fortunately, we came out of the fight better than Muhammad Ali's face (but not better than his pocket book)."

Sterling also bought the Cinerama, Southcenter, and Tacoma Mall theaters from United Theatres, one of Bill Forman's companies, in 1972. Then in 1976, they purchased the Roxy Theatre in Longview, the Liberty Theatre in Kelso, and the balance of stock in Your Drive-In in Port Angeles (which had been built in 1950). In April 1977, a swap meet opened in Pasco at the River-Vue Drive-In, a lease was approved to operate the West Tacoma multiplex, and two previously leased theaters, the Liberty and Capitol in Walla Walla, were purchased, all in 1977.

Roxy Theatre.

Your Drive-In announcing opening night.

Liberty Theatre, Walla Walla.

It was during this period that the company began the conceptual development process for the Sunset Drive-In property in Bellevue and purchased land across from the Alderwood Mall near Interstate 5 in Lynnwood for $960,000.

Long-time SRO booking department employee Roger Forbes approached Fred to operate an X-rated theater. Fred told him he wasn't interested in running such a theater but was willing to sell him the Garden Theatre in downtown Seattle. Forbes eventually turned his adult movie business into the Déjà Vu Strip Clubs.

In addition to the operations in California and Washington, Fred spread his reach into new areas. In 1973, rock band manager and promoter Larry Goldblatt tried to organize a song-writing contest in Saratoga Springs, New York, with the support of local businesses. The American Song Festival fell apart so Goldblatt approached Sterling in his hometown of Seattle. "Festivals are needed because there are thousands and thousands of song writers who don't know how to get their songs listened to," Goldblatt told the *New York Times*.[4] He thought that songwriters could circumvent the highly commercial set of criteria imposed by the record companies. Sterling bought the contest and appointed Malcolm C. Klein as the president. Instead of having authors perform their songs, Goldblatt recruited name performers. Income came from author entrance fees ($10.85), a share of ticket sales, and sales of a record with all the finalists' songs. The first winner took home $30,500 and a grand piano. The following year, the contest moved from Saratoga Springs to Hollywood, but without Goldblatt. Sterling owned the contest for ten years, and Tad participated in operating the contest, first as vice president and then as president of the organization for about eight years. As of 2010, the contest was still operating.

On the internal side of the company, Third & University Corporation was dissolved with the Palomar building and land being transferred to Sterling Theatres. Progressive Company was dissolved, as was Sterling Men's Wear Company (created by John in 1915). Sterling Men's Wear continued to operate as a California corporation. All these assets transferred to the management of Sterling Theatres through the trusts.

Fred's staff noted that the name Sterling Theatres did not really capture the scope of the work they were doing in radio stations, bowling centers, swap meets, and real estate. In June 1973, the board of directors renamed the company Sterling Recreation Organization. When Sterling Theatres Co. (formerly Granada Theatre Co.) was liquidated in March of 1976, the Sterling Theatres name remained alive by changing Sterling Realty Co. to Sterling Theatres. It can be very confusing

4   John Rockwell, "36 Songs Vie for a Festival's Prizes," New York Times, August 30, 1974, 22.

to figure out what is meant when Sterling Theatres is used in a formal sense unless you know what time period is being referenced.

The offices of Sterling Theatres finally moved out of Seattle in 1973. Much of the company's work now was outside of Seattle, and Bellevue was a less expensive place to operate a business. John Danz had originally planned to build a second floor above the lobby of the theater that eventually bore his name. In 1972, Fred had that floor constructed, and it became the John Danz Building. The offices moved to the John Danz Building, 600 106th Northeast on May 21, 1973. As the company grew over the next few years, it became necessary to take office space in various other buildings in Bellevue, always within walking distance of the administrative offices.

John Danz Building—second floor added over theater lobby.

By the middle of the 1970s, Fred's marriage to Selma had come to an end. A new relationship bloomed soon after, and on March 15, 1976, Fred and Bess Leigh Johnson were married.

Fred continued John's custom of giving back to the community, but the practice was highly individualized and very informal. Community organizations professionalized their development programs, and more not-for-profits approached Fred for support. The board of directors of Sterling Recreation established a charitable contribution limit of $5,000 for the company at the June 1977 board meeting. As far as I can determine, this was the first formal Charities Fund. There was no actual committee; Fred generally made all the decisions. On occasion, he discussed an idea with someone else, and from time to time, he asked me to help evaluate a proposal because I had several years of experience in fund raising, grant writing, and project analysis. Company contributions were concentrated in the areas of health, human services, and education and remain concentrated in those areas. In the last few years, the contributions committee added the areas of global warming and environmental impact to the list of grant eligibility.

In 1989, Fred had a discussion with David Schooler about the Bellevue Schools Foundation, whose board David had just joined. The Foundation was eight or nine years old at the time and had an annual budget of about $30,000. Fred wanted to know if David thought the foundation could put a half million dollars to good use. The contribution would be given over five years, there would be strings attached as to how it could be used, and it would require annual reporting. David was sure the foundation would be able to use such funds and put Fred in contact with the Bellevue Superintendent of Schools Don O'Neil. The school district and the foundation put together a proposal that was intended to assist students in the pre-kindergarten and post high school categories in an effort to help break the cycle of poverty. The proposal included the Danz Preschool, located in one of the elementary schools and a program of college scholarships. The Head Start model pre-school targeted about twenty low-income students a year, and the scholarship program gave out a total of fifteen scholarships over five years. Five of those scholarships were for four years each, one was for three years, eight were for two years, and one received a one-year scholarship.

The foundation tracked the pre-school program and continued it after the grant ran out. It was a terrific "feel good" endeavor, but they came up against two issues: What difference did the preschool make in the schools, and how many of the students stayed in the Bellevue schools? The preschool, surprisingly, seemed to make a very small difference in the overall success of the students, and the population was so highly mobile that an average of only three of the students were still attending Bellevue schools by the third grade. These revelations caused the Bellevue Schools Foundation not to renew the program.

At the time Fred offered the five-hundred-thousand-dollar contribution to the Bellevue Schools Foundation, he offered the same opportunity to the Lake Washington Schools Foundation. Unfortunately, it was never able to put together a program that Fred would approve so it received just one contribution of one hundred thousand dollars.

One of the things Fred wanted to happen was for the Bellevue Schools Foundation to grow. Today, in its fourth decade of operation, the budget of the foundation is about 1.5 million dollars annually. David Schooler says that Fred's efforts and this contribution through Sterling was the most significant step in a series of important steps that led to the foundation being one of the most successful in the state.

Fred, other members of the family, and executive staff members were able to meet some of the college scholarship recipients over the years. These were students who would not have been able to go to college without scholarships, and all in all, the program was extremely satisfying.

One recipient was admitted to the medical school at the University of Washington after completing his undergraduate work, and another had hoped to attend medical school but was not admitted. She had, however, become a dental assistant and then was admitted to dental school.

A third student graduated from the University of Washington with a BA in English and another in Chinese, studied abroad in Beijing and London, and went on to pursue a Master of Fine Arts degree at Amherst.

Another recipient became a ceramic engineer, and a fifth student graduated in International Business, receiving a Certificate of International Studies in Business with a concentration in marketing. One of David's most memorable encounters was with a student who had been called stupid and told she couldn't learn until she was able to participate in the tutoring program supported by the Bellevue Schools Foundation. Her tutor discovered that she was dyslexic, helped her learn how to learn, and when David heard her speak, she was on her way to college following a very successful high school career.

In the early 1990s, Fred was introduced to Heritage College (now Heritage University) and to its president, Sister Kathleen Ross, SNJM. He admired Sister Ross and her mission immensely and made regular contributions through the company to support her efforts. Other members of the family got involved over time supporting the school with both time and financial contributions. Barbara Danz Daniels served on the Heritage Board from 2000 to 2006 and was the prime mover in the creation of the Danz Family Endowment Fund at Heritage, which at the end of 2010, was valued at more than $70,000. Barbara hopes that the fund will be increased until it holds at least one hundred thousand dollars, at which time there should be enough funds to maintain the balance while offering annual scholarships to Heritage students.

I have just (2010) completed my first three-year term as a member of the Heritage Board of Directors, and Barbara and I were very pleased to be asked to give the invocation at the inauguration of the second president of Heritage University, Dr. John Bassett, in early November of 2010.

Barbara currently participates with the Community Day School Association in Seattle, and Penny has been part of the Seattle Art Museum support group for several years. Through our work with these and other community organizations, my sisters and I feel that it is an honor to carry on the tradition of giving back to the community demonstrated by our grandmother.

Through his personal foundation, distinct from the Charities Fund, Fred contributed to dozens of causes every year. In 2000 alone, he contributed to forty-four different charitable organizations.

Today the company gives about 5 percent of its profits back to the community every year, mostly under the auspices of the Charities Committee, on which family members and the company president serve. In addition, the company will match charitable contributions made by family members or staff up to a specified limit.

The company also started providing scholarships to employees in the 1980s. They could apply for up to $250 per year to help pay for tuition and books originally, but the amount was increased to $1000 in 1992. The courses ideally had a general connection to the employee's either current or anticipated duties with the company.

Fred was personally involved in a great many community projects. He was one of the very early participants in establishing the Eastside Community Mental Health Center, pushed to establish a hospital in the community, was one of the early board members of Overlake Hospital, served for many years on the Overlake Hospital Foundation Board, was a leader of the local Variety Tent, helped establish the Bellevue Downtown Park, and was a member of dozens of other non-profit boards of directors, city advisory committees, and special project advisory groups.

Under Fred's command, the company was growing and flourishing with profits increasing. The financial statements show that between 1965 and 1970 the assets of Sterling Theatre Co. and affiliates more than doubled.

Transformation

❧ 1978–1989 ❧

By 1978, the company had plans for major expansion, building new theaters, but was having difficulty getting projects permitted. Cities all over the world were beginning to examine more carefully how their communities were growing and were subjecting building proposals to approval by "urban planners." John Danz had needed only to submit his blueprints to the building department, pay the fee for the building permit (or maybe just pay a fee), and he was on his way. Things were more complex now, and projects stalled for want of proper planning. The answer to this problem was young David Schooler.

David was raised in Chicago and received his BA and a masters in Urban and Regional Planning from the University of Wisconsin. He then went to earn a law degree at the University of Denver in order to become a better city planner. While doing his laundry at a cousin's home in Denver he met a young woman named Kristen Webb who had come over from next door to borrow sugar. As a romance began to form and crystalize between them, David told her she could not expect him ever to make much more than about thirty thousand dollars a year in his chosen profession, helping communities plan their future. She must have been willing to accept that fate because she married him anyway.

David Schooler

They chose to settle in Seattle where Kristen could be near her parents in Ellensburg. David secured a position with the planning department at the City of Bellevue as the city's first legal planner.

After a couple of years, he was ready for a change and started looking for a new position. Jerry Vitus, Sterling Recreation's general manager, offered him a job with a starting salary of $22,000 a year, which was what Fred had approved. David said no thank you because that was what he was earning at the city. Jerry offered $24,000. David and Kristen were leaving the next day for a vacation to Arizona and Mexico so David told Jerry he would think about the offer. He called from the airport the next day to accept the position and started work at Sterling Recreation on January 19, 1979 when he was twenty-nine years old.

Jerry Vitus, General Manager of Sterling Recreation Organization pictured with Sidney Pollack, Director of 1982 film Tootsie

David Schooler's mission was to get theaters designed, permitted, and built. His first project was a basic theater in the south end of Bellingham called the Sehome. It employed a design for a very basic triplex that the Sterling staff called "the clone."

While this project was under way, Fred heard that AMC wanted to build a theater across the street from the Factoria property in Bellevue, which had been the site of the now closed Sunset Drive-In Theatre. Fred quickly scrapped the original project planned for Factoria that included building both a theater and an office building. In its place, they plopped down another clone because that was the fastest thing they could build. The idea was to be the first to open and scare AMC from building across the street. The theater opened in 1980 with a film called *The Big Red One*, starring Lee Marvin, Mark Hamill, and Robert Carradine, and the operation was a success from the beginning. David recalls that at opening night there were only about five empty seats among the three auditoriums.

The next project was a five-screen theater at the Alderwood Mall in Lynnwood. They had used a different form of low voltage lighting along the aisles in the Factoria Theatre called Tivo Lites. They worked out so well that they used them again at the Grand Cinemas Alderwood, but not just in the aisles. Tivo Lites went into the ceiling in the lobby. People loved it—the appearance, the movement—there was nothing else like it. Operations manager Bob Bond took the simple clone theaters and gave the houses some character. They were different, and it was an event to go out to them.

In 1982, the company launched a plan to add two more auditoriums at Factoria, one with six hundred and one with three hundred seats. Bob Hazard, Sterling's long-time film buyer announced in May that he had already booked a picture for Christmas, so the building had to be ready. They hustled and got things done very quickly. Fred, who was in charge of most everything, looked at the designs, but there was one detail he didn't focus on. The architects designed a ribbed arch that ran the length of the lobby. It had strips of mirror in it, a big mirror at the end, and strips of neon lights across the vault that seemed to move.

They reopened Factoria with five auditoriums in time for the Christmas season with *The Trail of the Pink Panther*, starring Peter Sellers and David Niven, in the new large auditorium. The multi-colored neon lights pulsed and bounced off the mirror at the back end of the vault. It was the first time that neon lights had been used in theater architecture since the 1930s, and it was a very exciting element in a simple design.

Robert Hazard, director of SRO Programming Department, with Fred Danz.

Fred loved it. Of course he never said that he loved it; he said it was good. In his vernacular that meant that you had done something spectacular.

Three more screens were added about two years later, going from five to eight. For many years, Factoria was the most successful theater in Puget Sound. A few years later, when it was operated by Cineplex, it was the fourteenth highest grossing theater in the United States.

All of Fred's children were serving as members of the board of directors by the early 1970s. Laurie's husband, Dick Hamlin was also an executive with the company. Tad, who was living in Southern California, commuted to Seattle to attend board meetings or, when necessary, participated by phone. When Matt Appelman retired in 1978, Tad took over the Southern California operations. In 1980, Tad was promoted to vice president of administration for Sterling Recreation and started commuting from Los Angeles to work in Bellevue. Usually he flew up on Monday and returned home on Friday. On April 7, 1983, the Board elected him president and chief operating officer (COO) with Fred retaining the position of chairman of the board and chief executive officer (CEO).

Tad Danz, president of Sterling Recreation Organization, 1984.

The arrangement was fraught with problems endemic to the company built by John Danz and inherited by Fred. Tad was very smart and had many ideas that he was keen to implement. Fred had been in sole charge of the company for twenty years, and it was definitely *his* company. Their management styles differed. David Schooler said, "Tad is very smart, highly analytical, very quick to decide, willing to take significant risk. More black and white than his dad. He was sometimes hard for other people to work for. And he worked hard, he worked very hard."

There were some difficult issues that could not be overcome. For example, Tad's wife and two children lived in California. Barbara was a partner in a major accounting firm. Daughter Leslie was eight in 1980, Greg was just five, and they had lived all their lives in Southern California. Barbara and the children were not interested in relocating to the Northwest.

One of the conflicts between Fred and Tad involved cigars. Tad liked to smoke cigars, and he smoked a lot of them. Fred, whose office was located next to Tad's, couldn't stand the smell of cigars and said so. Tad tried installing smoke eaters in the office. That didn't work very well. Finally, even though Tad was the president, Fred officially banned cigars in the office. The only person really affected by the edict was Tad. From then on, when Tad wanted a smoke, he had to go sit in his car and work.

Out of the blue in 1984, Fred called Tad into his office and told him that the commuting arrangement was not working. Tad's schedule made it difficult for him to be fully present as company president. In addition, and even more important, it was impossible for Tad to be the kind of husband or father he wanted and needed to be when he was absent from home most of the week. Fred fired his son for the second time.

On November 30, 1984, Tad officially resigned from all Sterling Recreation related positions except for his seat on the board of directors. He and Fred worked out an arrangement whereby Tad purchased several Southern California properties, including the La Mirada Drive-In and Swap Meet, the Parkway Bowl (a very modern bowl in a good location in El Cajon), the La Mesa Bowl, and the College Theatre. They agreed on a price they both believed represented proper values, but no formal appraisal was done. These were all properties owned by the trusts, and John's will stipulated that the two grandsons should have the opportunity to own trust properties with the company carrying the debt and that they could pay for the purchase over time from the revenues. Tad returned to his family and built his California enterprises into an even more successful operation.

Earlier in the year, Fred's daughter Laurie Hamlin, preferring to be in business by herself rather than with the family, had purchased the Sunset Village Shopping Center from the company using her Sterling shares. The purchase price was based on an appraisal of the ground lease that Fred had entered into with Nikum in 1960, twenty-two years earlier. Laurie and her husband, Dick, then both resigned from the board of Sterling Recreation on July 25, 1984.

When Tad purchased the Southern California properties without an appraisal, Laurie filed a lawsuit against Fred for acting less than judiciously as trustee. This was very distressing to Fred, so much so that for several months he seldom came into the office. At one point when David Schooler went to his home to deliver some papers, Fred's wife, Bess, met him at the door and commented how Laurie's lawsuit was very hard on him. The case went on for a long time but was finally settled without going to court.

On February 6, 1985, Fred's family and the staff of Sterling surprised him on the occasion of the fiftieth anniversary of his employment with Sterling. He had first started work in the theaters at the age of sixteen. The staff had secretly organized a huge cocktail reception and dinner in the Spanish Ballroom for somewhere around four hundred guests. Invitations featured a TOP SECRET message and, "Shhh, not a word to Fred." This was just about the only time anyone was able to put together a surprise for Fred, or keep anything from his knowledge. Only when he walked into the lobby of the Olympic Hotel on what he thought was a dinner date with Bess did he see the sign for SRO and realize that something was up. The surprise bowled him over; Bess teasingly wanted to know what else he might not know. Keeping

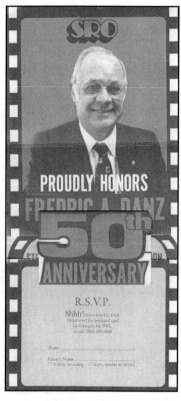

Invitation to Fred Danz's
surprise party
February 6, 1985.

anything from Fred had always been considered impossible.

Several speakers from far and near roasted and toasted Fred. There were guests from the Hollywood community, representatives from the distributors (David thinks perhaps from Warner Brothers and Paramount), and representatives from the national Variety Club organization. Some of the theater managers, the division managers, executive staff, and hundreds of friends, family members, and business associates joined the celebration.

The 1980s continued to be a turbulent decade for Sterling Recreation Organization. The first half focused on expansion in all areas. Changes in the federal tax code triggered a building boom in Seattle and other major cities. This added to a national trend of growth in "edge cities" like Bellevue—which was on one major freeway and between two others—and skylines shot up like shiny, cubical mushrooms. Sterling's holdings placed it in an ideal position to expand further and to benefit.

Company growth was so significant in California that Fred found himself traveling south more often, warranting the purchase of an apartment for him in Los Angeles. He could spend time in the region in comfort and without the expense and annoyance of hotels.

Among the California expansion properties of the early 80s were new theaters (the Baldwin Hills Theatre complex and the Carriage Square Theatre in Oxnard), three new bowling centers (20th Century

Bowl, Gateway Lanes, and West Park Lanes), plus ten acres of land acquired adjacent to the Bakersfield Swap-o-Rama.

In the Northwest, the company acquired the land under the John Danz Theatre from Rainier Theatre Company, which was wholly owned by the trusts. John Danz had purchased the land and had never relinquished his personal ownership of the parcel under the theater. Four more theaters came into the chain, including one eight-screen and one six-screen project in Portland and the Lyons Avenue four-plex in Spokane. The Uptown Theatre in Richland was rebuilt as a triplex, and four more screens were added to the Lewis & Clark in Tukwila.

Continuing with the trend of expansion, a four-plex theater went up on seven acres of land in Kelso, and another triplex on the Jefferson School site in Walla Walla received approval. Two new auditoriums were added to the Viking Twin in Bellingham, and the entire building was remodeled.

Building theaters gave the company expertise in site planning, architecture, permitting, construction, and building operation and maintenance, and the organization had mastered the needs of facilities that saw heavy use. In addition, since the days of the Palomar in downtown Seattle (and even earlier), some theater buildings included office and retail space rented to other tenants who were often far easier on the property than tens of thousands of movie fans and decidedly easier to manage. Sterling owned several pieces of suburban property that held promise as sites for office buildings or other development. As the region grew, businesses and corporations that once had Seattle addresses looked for more and cheaper space, closer to the residences of executives and employees and proximate to the network of interstate highways.

For quite some time, Fred had been talking to a number of developers about building a Class A high-rise office building on the downtown Bellevue property. Class A buildings represent the highest quality buildings in their market—they are the best looking, have the best construction with high quality building infrastructure, are well located with good access, are professionally managed, and command the highest rents. As David told me,

> [Fred] was holding out for a 10 percent return on one hundred dollars a foot. We had paid five dollars a foot not too many years before. Fred became convinced that Jon Runstad and Jon Nordby [of the well-known Seattle area commercial real estate development company Wright Runstad] would be the best suited for Sterling Recreation. Negotiating the lease was long and was the first time any of us had negotiated a deal of this kind. We flew Jim Graaskamp out to consult with us about how to structure the lease.

Jim was the head of the Real Estate Department at the University of Wisconsin. Although he was a quadriplegic, he had a national consulting practice. David said Graaskamp is one of the smartest people he has ever met, and the weekend was one of the most energizing periods of time those participating ever experienced. What he laid out was exactly what was used for both the Bellevue Two Center building (now the Symetra Tower) and for the next building, the Key Center.

At the time the Two Bellevue Center building was started, there was some consideration being given to a plan to visually tie together the Sterling Recreation property with the other end of the super block where One Bellevue Center, the Puget Power building, is located. Eventually, it was decided that the nature of the two owners, a regulated utility and a privately held company, were so different that their interests would most likely not line up well. However, because of that early idea, the buildings look similar. They were originally called One Bellevue Center and Two Bellevue Center (although Fred never wanted to be "two" of anything). If you look closely, you can see that the ground floor plazas of the two buildings line up.

In order to start construction of Two Bellevue Center, the developers needed pre-leasing for about 35 percent of the building and were having trouble getting there. On hearing this, Fred agreed to take the entire sixteenth floor. When the twenty-five-story building was completed in 1986, the executive offices moved into very elegant office space next door. Accounting, computer services, and various other departments stayed in the offices in the John Danz Building.

Two Bellevue Center, later Symetra Tower.

About the middle of the 1980s, Fred decided it was time to expand at Northgate. He believed that having one big theater in the Northgate market wasn't enough. He wanted more screens before somebody else built them. David received the job of finding the land on which to build a new theater. He spent time inspecting, researching, and analyzing several different options. Then he got a call from broker Roland Jones. The Rainier Fund had just leased the Oak Tree School site (land once owned by Seattle pioneer David Denny on Aurora Avenue North) from the Seattle School District. A new grocery store was going in there, and Jones thought a theater would be a great addition to the development. They asked $125,000 a year for a ground lease.

The idea created a great deal of excitement in the office. Under the Seattle parking code, they could build a two-thousand-seat theater building. Following the success of the Factoria Cinemas the company had a taste for building things with a little more panache. Fred was thrilled but insisted on multiple pro forma (a financial model using parameters such as income, vacancy rates, various expenses, and other details to test possible outcomes) being created to prove the feasibility of the project. Before a deal was completed, Bob Parks of the Rainier Fund called to say that costs had risen considerably and they would need $150,000 a year. David was afraid to tell Fred that he couldn't get the site for the $125,000 anymore. After more negotiations, they managed to split the difference and got the lease for $135,000.

The project went ahead using Olson Sundberg as architects (later winner of the 2009 AIA Architecture Firm Award). Olson had done residential and some museums, but this may have been their only theater. They designed a wonderful building with a vaulted lobby and an island bar, which was unusual in theaters in those days. Lots of neon and metal lit up the design. When grocery store owner Larry McKinney saw what was being done at the theater, he changed the look of his store. This was the first big Larry's Market and the first of its kind in Puget Sound with a deli bar, salad bar, gourmet aisle, and a staffed seafood department. A grocery and theater sharing a parking lot was unusual at the time.

When the Oak Tree Cinemas opened, it was a great success, hitting pro forma numbers the first year and percentage rent by the second year. Rents are set in the lease, but sometimes a requirement is added that provides for additional rent once a specific level of income is achieved. Typically, the percentage applies to sales or other income in excess of a pre-established base amount.

Oak Tree Cinemas.

❦ ❧

In the mid-1970s, Sony, JVC, and Phillips introduced videocassette recorders, allowing viewers at home to "time shift"—tape television programs when they aired and watch them later. Viewers could also play their favorite movies without the trouble of traveling to a theater and the expense of tickets. The television and motion picture industries filed suit to block this technology as an infringement on their copyrights, but in 1984, the Supreme Court of the United States held that there was no infringement when videos were shown in the home. A new industry was born, or at least legalized.

Although viewing movies at home potentially cut into Sterling's box office revenues, it was time to engage the new technology. In June 1985, Sterling began selling videocassettes of popular films in the lobby of the Lewis & Clark seven-plex. Patrons could go home with their favorite movies and play them back whenever they wanted. The experiment proved a success, and Fred had his friend Lou Laventhal (who operated several video sales locations) open a store at the Lewis & Clark at the end of the year. In January 1986, the company's first video store went into the Grand Cinemas Alderwood, and the Lewis & Clark outlet soon became a Sterling-operated store. Fred asked

Ted Daniels (the husband of Bill's daughter Barbara) to work on the video stores project. Ted traveled to research the field and discovered that super stores were beginning to open around the country. Ted recommended that the video stores be separated from the theaters. When the Oak Tree opened, a video store was also opened in the retail section of the Oak Tree Center, separate from the theater. Ted and then Paul Bern managed the video stores until Mike Lancaster took over the operation.

During the second half of the 1980s, Sterling began expansion in a new direction by starting to develop some of the land they held. One of the first new projects was the Tacoma South Shopping Center, a 170,000-square-foot project with Associated Grocers and Drug Emporium as anchor tenants and a multiplex theater. In 2003, when the theater lease was not renewed, the building was remodeled into a Pure Fitness Health Club facility. In 2006, the grocery space was replaced by a Lowe's home improvement store.

The next project continued development of the original Sunset Drive-In Theatre site with the 1989 construction of a six-story, 130,000-square-foot office building called Sterling Plaza near the Factoria Theatre. An existing building next to Sterling Plaza, which we simply call the 12600 Building, was purchased in 1996. This building is two stories and 52,000 square feet.

Sterling Plaza.

12600 Building.

It was time for the five-year lease on the Sterling offices in the Two Bellevue Center building (by then the Rainier Tower) to be renewed. During the entire span of the lease, Fred had complained that the rent was too high, and when it came time to renegotiate the lease, Sterling asked for a reduction. Wright Runstad declined. Sterling gave notice that they were moving, and David Schooler went looking. He soon found the two-story, thirty-thousand-square-foot Atrium Building just two blocks away. When Wright Runstad learned the company was planning to vacate the entire floor, they offered a better deal, and Fred, who really enjoyed the wonderful space he was occupying in the Rainier Tower, agreed to stay. David thought the Atrium Building was a pretty nice building, but Fred never really liked it, so it was sold in 1999. Just before the sale closed, there was an announcement that an apartment building was going to be built next door which would have blocked some of the pleasant views from the building, so no one was very sad to see the building go.

A third project involved the 1990 development of an old theater site in Bellingham, Washington, into a forty-three-thousand-square-foot strip mall with Ross Dress for Less as its anchor tenant.

The first of two storage facilities came into the mix of commercial properties in 1991 with the purchase of a mini storage facility in Arlington, Washington. Six years later, an addition increased capacity from 405 to 539 units. Also in 1997, a second storage facility was included in the purchase of a thirty-nine-thousand-square-foot retail center in Spokane, adding another 418 units of mini storage.

A natural adjunct to owning and operating radio stations was also to own the transmission towers. As early as 1981, the company purchased a transmission site in Oregon, in 1983 purchased a site outside of Denver, and in 1988 added another Colorado site, the Lee Hill tower. Another tower was added in the West Seattle area, and as office buildings were built, transmission sites were placed on the roofs of the taller buildings. These various sites are also the location for ambulance, police, and other emergency services, as well as a variety of non-emergency communications transmissions.

West Seattle transmission site.

The first half of the 1980s was marked by the biggest expansion in the history of the company. By 1986, the organization operated 116 screens (see Appendix B).

Then the second half of the decade saw contraction and consolidation of all the operating units. What changed? I think there were a number of factors that influenced Fred's decision.

Fred had been struggling for many years with the question of how to transfer the company and the wealth held within it to the third generation.

Another significant consideration for Fred was most likely the great expense of running so large an organization made up of so many operating units coupled with a relatively small profit margin. In addition to the hardtop theaters and drive-ins, there were the swap meets, radio stations, bowling centers, video stores, storage facilities, communication towers, as well as other smaller businesses.

Among the many facilities and one of the smallest, was an in-house facility called "the Shop"—which was responsible for physical and technical support to the organization. Its employees made keys, repaired equipment, and in general handled issues of maintenance in the theaters, bowls, and radio station. They also produced graphics for the various units. Sterling owned the video machines and arcade games that were in the theaters and bowls with a fellow named Bill Clark as the head of the Games Division. The Shop maintained the arcade and video games too. Don Dvorak was the equivalent of our chief engineer for decades.

Curt & Norm working in the Shop

Don Dvorak started working at the Florence Theatre in June of 1929 as a projectionist and stayed for more than fifty years, working in many different theaters, becoming chief projectionist in 1953 for Washington, California, and Oregon. He was honored by the company at a banquet in 1979 at the Washington Plaza Hotel, celebrating his fifty years with the company.

Don Dvorak celebrated his fiftieth year with SRO.

Ushers, managers, cashiers, a large accounting office (taxes, accounts receivable, accounts payable, internal auditing, etc.), public relations, advertising, and numerous other positions had to get checks every payday. More than two thousand employees supported the various operating units. The entire business was both labor and capital intensive. The profit margins remained narrow and subject to the whims of the economy and patrons' access to disposable income for entertainment. At the same time, all over the country there was a race on among the theater exhibitors to build bigger, fancier, and more expensive theater complexes. Multiplexes went from two to four to six until they finally got to eighteen or twenty or more. At the same time taste in theatrical exhibition, screens, sound systems, aspect ratios, and seating (going from smooth canted floors to stepped auditoriums) changed. There was a great deal of new construction replacing older plants that were then required to be kept on a company's books for twenty or more years. With the costs of labor, film purchasing, popcorn, and maintenance … a lot of theater companies went out of business. Moving older theaters from first-run to second- or third-run to dollar houses wouldn't make enough to be profitable. The capital expenses incurred in this expansion eventually caused the bankruptcy of about half of the motion picture exhibitors. Fred saw all this coming, and when the Reagan administration lifted the Paramount Decree (in a trend toward deregulation), there was a rapid run up in the value of theaters. The confluence of all these trends put Fred in a good position to sell.

Fred believed that operating the entertainment businesses required somebody at the head of the company who was blood—who would be vitally interested in the day-to-day working of the businesses. When Tad left the company, Fred could not see any other family member who might be able to take over for him. At sixty-eight, he and Bess were ready to take life a little easier, travel more, and spend more time together. He was already in the early stages of congestive heart failure and had undergone two open-heart surgeries. As early as 1977, Fred was interested in simplifying the structure of the organization and in estate planning. The directors began discussing consolidation of the Sterling Recreation companies by merging those owned by the same entity (i.e., SRO, Sterling Theatres Co., the trusts).

Fred settled on a consolidation plan of selling or combining businesses until there were no recreation companies left and then planned to get consent from all the ultimate beneficiaries and ask the court to allow the dissolution of the trusts.

The process was complicated. Some properties were owned by Fred as his separate property, some by the trusts, some by Capital Amusement Company (the executive retirement plan company), and John and Jessie's trusts each had separate provisions including different ownership percentages for beneficiaries. Consolidation produced many painful complications, including two either threatened or actual lawsuits from stockholders objecting to how the consolidation plan was executed and how properties and stock were valued.

In the process of simplifying the ownership structure, a dozen or more companies were merged into two—Columbia Theatre Company (the trusts) and Sterling Recreation Organization. A dissenters' rights suit was brought under state law over this merging of entities and had to be settled before the plan could move forward. There was also an issue about how the value of the dissent would be set. There was a major blow-up over the ownership of the basketball tickets the company had purchased for many years and endless negotiations over the ultimate buyout of those stockholders choosing to cash in their stock rather than participate with other family members in the ownership of the company.

A great deal of psychic pain and anxiety was caused as each sale of all or part of an operating unit meant losing staff (although many positions moved with the sold units). In 1984, the California theaters were sold to Pacific Theatres, Michael Forman's company (Bill Forman had died on April 29, 1981). The rest of the theaters—ninety-nine indoor screens and fifteen outdoor screens at thirty-nine locations—were leased or sold to Cineplex Odeon for $45.5 million in 1986, as were all except two of the radio stations in 1986. The video stores went on the block in 1992, and the assets of Capitol Amusement, the holding company for the executive retirement program, were liquidated. The executives who held shares split the proceeds. When Capitol Amusement was liquidated, there were twenty-seven participants (not including Fred and SRO); those who had been involved the longest realized almost a half million dollars, and the person who had been the last to participate, $1300. Between 1986 and 1992, the number of employees on the Sterling Recreation payroll went from two thousand to fewer than twenty.

Closing theaters met with some objections from the movie-going public. David Schooler told the *Herald* of Everett, "We had a drive-in in Longview for a long time and it got to the point it wasn't making money. When we sold and closed it, there were more people in Longview complaining than the number who ever appeared on a Friday or Saturday night."

In 2011, more than twenty years later, people who had worked as teenagers in Sterling theaters offered their memories and the impact on them of the system built by John Danz and continued by Fred.

Russ Knudsen wrote:

My life at the John Danz Theater started in about 1979 with the release of *Star Trek the Motion Picture*. My dad (Daniel Knudsen, a King County police officer) had a moonlighting job at the John Danz as a security officer on Friday and Saturday nights. He was also enlisted as a general handyman. I would frequently go with him to his odd jobs at the theater so I spent a lot of time watching movies. I attribute my love for movies to this experience and can recite every line of *Star Trek the Motion Picture* as a result.

In January of 1984, I was to turn sixteen, so Ib Johansen asked my dad, "When is Russ going to come work for me?" I guess my fate was sealed at that moment. On my sixteenth birthday, I started my first job at the John Danz as an usher. Because of my dad's position at the theater and because I picked up on things very quickly, I moved into the concession bar after a few weeks. Eventually I was good enough to train new bar workers where I trained a new kid named Eric Nutting. Eric would later go on to marry my sister Dianne. Later I trained another new guy named André who went on to work for a company that produced the digital extras for the movie *Titanic* (he can be seen in the behind-the-scenes videos on the DVD).

After a few months or so working at the JD, I met my first girlfriend (Jill Chatterton). By then I was showing up to work early to pull weeds in the parking lot to earn a little extra money. One day, Ib came to me and asked if we would work at Factoria Cinemas for a while. There was a shake-up happening there, and they needed employees quickly. So Jill and I moved over to Factoria Cinemas, which was a five-plex at the time, but three more theaters were on the drawing board to turn the theater into an eight-plex. After a couple of weeks working at Factoria, I found out what shake-up meant. We had a mandatory meeting one day where Bob Bond and Paul Burn (district managers) were in attendance. This was strange. It was discovered (by my dad) that a majority of employees had been stealing from the till or the bar. The offer put on the table at the meeting was, "You can quit now and no charges will be filed, or we can prosecute you, and we know who you are." On that day, there were only a small handful of employees left as just about everyone quit right after the meeting. I ended up staying at Factoria Cinemas.

Life at Factoria was a little harder than the JD; more employees, more movies to keep track of, etc. I started as an usher and ticket taker. After two years of working at Factoria, in 1986, I left for school in Phoenix. By the time I came back for Christmas break, SRO had sold the theaters to Cineplex Odeon. I worked Christmas break for a few weeks, but it wasn't the same.

The only time I ever met Fred Danz was while working at Factoria Cinemas. I was recruited as a driver to take Bob Bond, Paul Bern, and Fred Danz over to a restaurant close to Factoria so they could have a meeting. After waiting in the car for about an hour, all three of them came stumbling out and piled in the car. It was at that point that I realized why I was a driver as they had all been drinking. That was one of the more interesting jobs I had.

And from Russ's sister Dianne Knudsen Nutting:

From the time I was a little girl, I had accompanied my father, Dan Knudsen, to the John Danz Theatre when he was working security or painting a wall in his spare time. When I was sixteen (May 1985), my dad marched me into the theater and introduced me to Ib Johansen, someone I credit to this day as a person who instilled [in me] the moral "the customer is always right." I didn't know it, but I was introduced to my future husband as well, Eric Nutting. We have been married twenty-two years now and have five kids!

One day during those formative years, Eric asked Mr. Fred Danz for a meeting. He was kind enough to entertain my husband and said yes. During the meeting, Eric told Mr. Danz about an idea to turn the movie theatre into a live dinner theatre. Mr. Danz nodded his head and said, "I don't see the theatre going in that direction, but thank you for your enthusiasm." When the theater closed down, it was a sad moment for us, but we will hold the memories of the Danz family and the theater in our memories fondly.

Russ and Dianne's sister Senta offers this anecdote of life as a theater employee:

I'm working my first day at John Danz and being the newbie, they have me do all the basic stuff, taking tickets, cleaning the floors, "trashing" the theaters. So after the movie ends we go in to clean up the theater before the next showing, and I'm in the upper balcony, working as fast as I can. I grab what feels like a large drink that is full. I do the newbie thing and grab it by the top. As I'm picking it up, the top pops off, and the "drink" falls all over my hands, the floor, and my outfit. I then realize that it's not pop ... it's a HUGE drink glass full of tobacco chew spit. Totally gross! I remember running back to the concession stand and going in the back room to the sinks and using the hottest water I could stand to burn off the gross chew.

I loved working at the John Danz, the big open floor, the huge theatre, Dad working the security on Friday and Saturday nights. It was the best first job I could have asked for.

Even Russ and Diane's father contributed some memories:

In the 1970s, I was hired as security for the John Danz Theatre in Bellevue. At that time, I wore a suit so as not to alert the patrons. I was a full-time King County sheriff and worked at the theater off duty.

As my son Russell got older and was looking for afterschool work, I encouraged him to apply at the theater, and he was hired as a ticket taker, cashier, and several other jobs. When my daughter Dianne reached her sixteenth birthday, she went to a movie with her mother, and I was working that day at the theater. Ib Johansen was the manager at that time, and he hired her on the spot, knowing that she would also be a good worker. Eric Nutting was a new hire and was taking tickets at the door. I looked over at him when Dianne was filling out employment papers, and well, to make a long story short, John Danz theater literally created another family. Eric and Dianne were married and now live in Florida with five fantastic children.

My youngest daughter Senta Knudsen also was interested in working part time and like her older brother and sister and father, she was hired and worked at the John Danz and Factoria theaters. As time went on, Dorothy, manager at the John Danz, had a pothole in the parking lot that was dangerous. I offered to repair that pothole. That job led me to [working as], I guess you would call me, a theater handyman. I repaired gold paint on the theater walls and stage re-paint. The Coke and other beverages were dispensed from boxes, and I created a cabinet system to hold the boxes. In a downtown Seattle theater, I built large boxes to hold popcorn bags, which had been stored loose.

One night I got a call from that same Seattle theater that was holding a rock concert. As part of the John Danz group, I did not hesitate to drive to the theater at 1:00 a.m. with my son Russ. We installed a 4 x 8 plywood sheet to the ticket window that was broken by concert goers.

I did think of John Danz as part of my family.

The social networking website Facebook includes a couple of fan pages for Sterling theaters which include these memories:

William Rahr Jr.: I sure enjoyed working there from 1973 to 1975. I made enough to go to Washington State University years one and two (go Cougs). I made a lot of friends and learned a lot about working with people and customers. I married the cashier, still am 36 years later. Still strong friends with Rick, Mike, John, and Steph. I miss Mike B. a lot.

Shannon Smith: I remember having to add up all the concession purchases in my head; makes me sick with envy to see these kids now with the registers doing all the work! I also remember the year *Indiana Jones* first came out. It was at Factoria with its tiny theaters. Meanwhile, at the gigantic John Danz, we had the first lame *Star Trek* or *Popeye* or something for weeks on end. Most days we were selling 100 or fewer seats.

❦ ❦

In an ironic footnote to Sterling's seventy-plus-year journey as an independent in the theater business, the company found itself on the wrong end of litigation over monopolistic bidding for bookings. Randy Finley, a former Sterling employee who started his own theater chain, sued Sterling and movie distributors, alleging that he and his small chain were excluded from top films by agreements that the big chains would take movies, good or bad. Exhibitors agreed not to compete with each other for films. The other big respondents, including General Cinema and UA Communications, settled with Finley, but Sterling went to trial. The jury verdict came down after Sterling got out of the theater business but still cost the company $6.6 million.

By 1992, all that remained of Sterling Recreation Organization was the land and the buildings, the telecommunication sites, two drive-in theaters, and a swap meet. The name of the company was changed on April 1, 1993, and Sterling Recreation Organization morphed into Sterling Realty Organization with ease. David Schooler, once in charge of the smallest unit of the company, became the president of the new organization in September of 1993.

David Schooler, President of Sterling Realty Organization

By the middle of the 1980s, the John and Jessie Danz trusts had been in effect for more than twenty years. Bill was seventy, and Fred was sixty-eight. The ultimate beneficiaries, the seven children of Bill and Fred who would eventually inherit the company, ranged in age from thirty-five to forty-seven. Most of us had children to care for and educate and some of us were single parents. All of us hoped to enjoy some of the wealth tied up in the trusts while we and our families were still young and healthy. Fred began exploring ways to transfer funds from the trusts to the beneficiaries to enhance our lives. He also began examining how best to abandon the trusts altogether.

The Next Century

❧ 1990–2011 ❧

The early part of the 1990s saw the final pieces of the consolidation of the company fall into place. The video division was sold in 1991 for $350,000 to Cianci's Videoland, and the bowling division in mid 1992 to Charan Enterprises for $2.8 million plus another $1.6 million for a non-compete agreement. Sterling, Fred, and Tad were not to open, purchase, or operate any bowling centers that might compete with the ones we were selling for a period of three years.

Belle Lanes Bowl in downtown Bellevue was not one of the bowling centers included in the sale to Charan. In the early nineties, David told Fred that he believed Belle Lanes, which was generating maybe $125,000 a year, could generate more cash flow if it was turned into a big box store. David had been doing research into other regional shopping centers and the stores located around them and found, for example, that there were a few big stores around Alderwood Mall. There were none in the area around Bellevue Square.

Fred and David engaged Colin Radford, a very good local broker (now a member of the SRO Board of Directors) to help. It took him quite a long time, but eventually he suggested a Texas company called Book Stop Book Star, owned by Leonard Riggio who had owned the Barnes & Noble name and its flagship Manhattan store since the 1970s. SRO signed an agreement with them to take over the entire Belle Lanes building, creating the largest bookstore they would have in the country.

During the negotiations, they decided this store would not be called Book Stop Book Star, but would carry the Barnes & Noble name. The negotiations were fairly easy, not very contentious, and pretty straightforward.

David recommended several local architects to help with the tenant improvements, and El Baylis was selected. David says he is a talented, engaging, soft-spoken gentleman. SRO was obligated to provide six hundred thousand dollars to redo the building, and the lessee was responsible to do the work and spend whatever was required in excess. One day, Mr. Baylis asked David to come down from his office next door (SRO's administrative offices were then located in the Rainier Tower building, now called Symetra Tower) to take a look at something.

The bowl had a suspended ceiling, and the building plans called for removal of the ceiling tiles, addition of air conditioning ducts, and raising the ceiling. At the time, they were bringing in gravel to fill the lane beds so that the floor would be all one level, so the air inside was choked with dust. However, what David saw was utterly remarkable beautiful cedar that made up the ceiling above the suspended tiles. Baylis said he thought they needed to keep the cedar ceiling and that it would not cost much to keep it. He also thought he could give the store interesting looking ducting. Baylis was able to convince Barnes & Noble to keep the ceiling, which is what you see today. Many people think it is rather eye popping.

Barnes & Noble ceiling from original bowl.

Belle Lanes Building transformed into Barnes & Noble.

They also decided that the grill, which was a very popular lunch spot and whose hamburgers Fred was very fond of, should be turned into some other kind of food shop. David had known a bookstore in Denver that had a coffee shop in it, and he suggested a coffee shop be put into the new B & N store. Company treasurer Tom Gilchrist suggested Starbucks. Barnes & Noble talked about the idea internally and decided not to go in that direction but remained uncertain about what they were going to do. They had already negotiated a percentage rent clause for the bookstore, and David and our attorney, Scott Osborne, thought it would be a good idea to leave the food area out of the percentage rent agreement because they believed the food area would be a drag on total earnings. David was even more convinced of this when the lessee called to say, "What would you think about us putting in a Honeybee Hams?" David replied, "Well, you'll sell a lot of ham sandwiches, but are you sure you want to be wholesaling hams out of your bookstore? Why don't you reconsider the Starbucks idea?" The man negotiating for Barnes & Noble responded that they had already talked about it in New York, and they really hadn't liked the idea, but he would try it again. About ten days later, he called David to say they had changed their minds. They had not only decided to put Starbucks in the Bellevue store, but they were going to put them in all of their stores. There would be no percentage rent of course—they had crossed it out. So our office has enjoyed the first Starbucks to be located in a Barnes & Noble bookstore just a few steps away.

Essentially, the company was now a commercial real estate organization, managing and developing its own properties. Property Management, the smallest division of Sterling Recreation Organization, was now the entire company. As each division was sold, the staff, including the division manager, also left. David Schooler was the last man standing.

❧ Portland ❧

David Schooler told me that the story of SRO development in Portland starts in Seattle in the early 1980s.

The biggest competition the company had then was Luxury Theatres owned by Tom Moyer who was expanding in Washington. He owned a good theater in Spokane, and in Seattle, he owned theaters, although not very good ones, in every significant Seattle submarket—downtown, south, east at Crossroads, near north side at Aurora, and in Everett. Most of his theaters were not very well built, nor were they well maintained. But he was starting to build more modern plants. He had been a good competitor for SRO, but David says, "We always had a better mousetrap." Moyer saw how successful some of the better designed places (like the our remodeled Uptown, Factoria, and Grand Cinemas Alderwood) were doing, and they built a new plant at Crossroads. When it opened, it was pretty snappy.

Fred knew he had to do something to keep ahead of the competition, so in 1983, David was given the task of studying the Portland theater market. He compared Portland to Seattle, San Diego, and Milwaukee and concluded that Portland was ripe for development of our theaters.

David traveled to Portland a number of times, looking for property, and eventually was shown the closed 82nd Avenue Drive-In, about ten acres in size. The road was pretty busy, the neighborhood looked like it would develop in the not too distant future, and the Johnson Creek freeway interchange was scheduled to go in soon. In addition, less than two miles south was a brand new regional shopping center built by one of the largest shopping center developers in the country. The drive-in property was owned by the Forman family, and Fred didn't want them to know who wanted to buy it. He took a page from his father's book and used Martin Peters as a "beard" who negotiated with the Formans to buy the 82nd Avenue property. Peters then immediately sold it to Sterling.

Fred was motivated to get something going in a hurry because the company was in a pretty tight competition in Seattle with Tom Moyer, and they wanted to do something in his backyard. As David said, "That would also be a punch in the nose." (Tom Moyer had been an AAU boxing champion.) With the assistance of our Portland agent, Michael Heerman (still our agent in the Portland area today), Sterling bought ten other parcels of land.

Johnson Creek Crossing, Portland.

Sterling needed a rezone of some of the residential properties to build the theater, but Fred wanted to get it up fast. Fred decided not wait for the rezone and moved ahead with a theater. Where they decided to put the theater was not the best place on the property with a shopping center around it, but it was the fastest thing they could do to compete with Tom Moyer.

They were in such a hurry that they decided to use the existing Oak Tree Theatre plans.

Most of the theaters SRO built in the Northwest were built by North Coast Construction, and on many sites, Fred Francel was the construction foreman in charge. Fred was a marvelous, tough professional, a good communicator, and a very, very practical person. This was all before building plans were digitized, and when the theater plans and site didn't match up with each other in quite the same way as they did in Seattle, we had to reverse the plans as if you had it in a mirror—what was on the left side had to be on the right side. Francel took the Oak Tree plans and tacked them up on the ceiling in the construction shack. He said, "Don't worry about it. It will work just fine for me." A building inspector would never go along with that today. The theater was still under construction in 1986 when the theaters were sold to Cineplex so a ground lease was created for the building.

By 1987, Sterling owned about seventeen acres at the development called Clackamas Crossing (later renamed Johnson Creek) but still hoped to expand all the way to Johnson Creek. Five or six years later, Mike Heerman finally found a woman who was willing to sell her property, but there were two problems. Fred didn't want to spend any money to acquire the land, and the woman wanted to live in the house for the rest of her life (she was about seventy-five).

Time for David to get creative. Sterling owned a site in Longview that was intended to be the future site for the Longview Twin Drive-In. It was so old that the culvert in it was made of wood. There was a problem with the property. The eruption of Mount St. Helens in 1980 had generated immense pyroclastic flows of mud and ice crashing down the Toutle River. The flooding had turned the Longview land into a wetland, which meant they couldn't do anything with it. Mike

Lancaster found a solution; he was able to work out an arrangement with a diking district in Longview to buy the site for water storage. The proceeds from that sale were used to buy the elderly woman's house in Portland together with a life estate. This parcel proved to be a critical piece because it enabled SRO to block another developer trying to create a development and purchase the same parcels Sterling was after. In the end, David made an agreement with the other developer in which they partnered to purchase the rest of the parcels to create a thirty-acre site right at the interchange.

It was at that time that big-box stores were coming into vogue. The traffic count was good, and development was coming up the street from Town Center. The plan required complicated arrangements: many parcels still had to be acquired, there were two streets and a school site that had to be vacated, and a sale of nine acres to Home Base needed to close, including a reciprocal easement and development agreement, all within one year, according to the terms of the very temporary development agreement. While they managed to get it all accomplished in time, a recession then stopped further development.

During the original development period, The Home Depot had tried to come in to the new center, but too late to stop an agreement with Home Base. When, after a few years, Home Base suffered a system-wide meltdown and closed many stores, The Home Depot turned its nearby store into a Wal-Mart and took over the Home Base store at Clackamas Crossing. Later in the nineties, a lease was signed with Pet Smart, but then there was no movement for a long time until Babies R Us signed a lease for a store in the south end of the shopping center, probably the biggest hole at the time. David says this was probably the most difficult lease negotiation he ever went through.

The next few years saw development of several of the pads—Burger King, a bank, Outback, and Starbucks, which was also a very difficult lease that took almost two years to negotiate. David thinks the most difficult leases are those where agreements are seemingly reached but when the next draft of the lease appears the terms are very different than what you thought were the previously agreed to terms.

In 1999, there was still one big hole between the theater and Babies that David was negotiating with Staples to fill. The Staples negotiation proved to be another extremely difficult one, and when Best Buy offered to lease, David did something he has rarely done. He changed horses in mid-stream. Negotiating with Best Buy proved to be one of the easiest letters of intent and one of the easiest leases he ever worked on. They were firm in what they wanted, and it was very easy and very quick to work through. The Best Buy store was ready to open in 2000.

When Cineplex went broke, it sold or transferred the Portland location to Regal Theaters, which also went bankrupt. In that bankruptcy, SRO agreed that they would continue at the same rent, but each party had the ability to terminate the lease with six months' notice. When Regal decided to reinvest at the nearby Clackamas Town Center and significantly upgrade that theater, which made our theater a secondary one, Regal decided to close. Fortunately, at the same time, GI Joe's was looking for a spot. David had talked with them over the years about being at Johnson Creek, and this time it worked out. He found them very good to work with—they were adamant in that they knew what they had to do and wanted from us, but they were easy to work with. The theater building was torn down, and a new GI Joe's store replaced Regal Cinemas in 2004.

When GI Joe's went bankrupt, we were left with a good-sized hole. That was at the beginning of the recession that began in 2008. We were approached in early 2008 by Dicks Sporting Goods to go in that spot in a long, difficult negotiation, but David got the deal done, and Dicks opened before Thanksgiving 2010. SRO ended up with a very good center, including what is believed to be both the second best Home Depot and Best Buy in the Portland market.

⸙

In the fall of 1992, in preparation for the eventual distributions of the trusts and the transfer of majority ownership to the third generation, Barbara, Penny, and I all were elected to SRO's board of directors, joining Alison and Tad. By the middle of the decade, the mergers and consolidation were complete, and as all of the ultimate beneficiaries of the trusts were in agreement that the trusts should be ended, Fred went to a judge. With the approval of the court, the trusts were finally distributed in 1998.

There were, in effect, seven of us who now owned significant percentages of the company, plus a smaller but still significant percentage owned by Fred. Of course, each of the two male beneficiaries owned twice as much as any one of the women. Tad, Rian, and Laurie all chose not to participate with the other four cousins in the business, so we arranged to buy out their shares. (Tad kept shares he previously owned). Once accomplished, the four women, Barbara Danz Daniels, Carolee Danz, Penny Danz Coe, and Alison Danz became the majority owners of Sterling Realty Organization, the newest iteration of the original Sterling Theatres Company.

We not only participated as board members, but we also formed the nucleus of the Charities Committee. Our allocation of funds had now grown in size, allowing us to contribute significant funds to the community every year, somewhere in the neighborhood of $250,000. Previously Fred had made all the decisions about where to contribute although from time to time he asked me to research a proposal for him, confer on a donation decision, or attend a few grant-maker conferences on his behalf. The new members of the Charities Committee agreed to continue to fund requests in the same areas of concern on which Fred had focused: health, human services, and education.

I think there is a touch of irony in the way things worked out. John and Fred had both assumed the company would continue to be operated by family members, but I doubt if either of them ever considered that it would be in the control of four women of the third generation. Of course, when this occurred Fred accepted the reality with his usual aplomb.

In the summer of 1999, Fred found it necessary to undergo a third heart surgery. He spoke to Alison and to me, asking if we would be willing to become interim co-chairwomen until he was recovered enough to return. As always, he wanted to be sure that there was family oversight and participation in the decision-making process. I think he was also trying to maintain a balance between the two families—his own and Bill's—in his decision to recruit one from each. I had just left a position as the interim director of the Bellevue Community College Foundation with no expectation of returning to work but agreed to participate while Fred was gone. While there was no way Alison and I would be able to fill even one of Fred's shoes, he knew that he had excellent senior officers in place with President David Schooler, who had been part of Sterling for twenty years, and Vice President Tom Gilchrist, who had originally joined Sterling in 1983 as a tax accountant.

Tom Gilchrist, was raised in Bellevue and went to Washington State University where he had been a very good baseball pitcher. He was even drafted by the Cleveland Indians in 1979. He says it would have been kind of fun to sign, but at the time, he was going out with Nancy, and he was in love. Besides, it didn't seem like the prudent thing to do. In hindsight, he continues, it would have been interesting to see if he could have made it. He played two years at WSU and then ended up quitting baseball.

Tom Gilchrist, SRO vice president and treasurer.

After graduating from WSU in 1983, he moved back to Bellevue with his wife, Nancy. Tom told me that he was having a great time golfing every day while Nancy worked as a teacher. On a Monday morning after about two weeks of this, as she headed out to work and he was lolling around watching TV, she informed him, "You need to get a job."

So Tom said OK and, looking in the paper, found Pace Employment, which was located in the Paccar building in downtown Bellevue. They sent him first to apply for a job in the Rainier Valley

> which was basically a check cashing place where you had shotguns … it was a little out of my comfort zone so I went back to Pace and told them that doesn't really work.

They told Tom that there was an opening across the street at a company called Sterling Recreation, "the movie theater guys." They were able to see Tom right away so he walked across the street and interviewed with Janice Webb, supervisor in theater bookkeeping.

> We talked for an hour and a half. She was also a "Coug," and we kind of hit it off. When I got home, she called and said they would like to hire me for $5.00 an hour. "Can you start tomorrow?" So my wife came home, and I said OK, I got a job. She was happy.

When Tom went to work for Janice as a theater bookkeeper in June of 1983, he didn't know how to use a ten-key. Dave Chandler, the assistant controller, used to sit in a glass cubicle overlooking the accounting department, and Tom said,

> You felt like Dave was watching you all the time. Every time he would come by, I would just start pounding random numbers on the ten-key because I didn't want him to know that I didn't know how to use it.

Tom had worked for Janice for only a few months when Myron Banwart, who was controller, said he wanted Tom to change positions.

At the time, there was a six-month requirement before an employee could change jobs so they had to get corporate authorization to have Tom move into the tax department, where he went to work for Gary McGrath. Tom was doing business taxes and sales taxes, then soon became tax accountant when Peg Phillips left to take a role in the television series *Northern Exposure* (as the old lady store owner).

Gary McGrath, controller.

Tom did various levels of taxes. He started with sales taxes and business and occupation taxes and then went to income taxes. The company dealt with all sorts of taxes because it had not only the various corporate taxes but also the trusts, Fred's individual taxes, and several different partnership returns. Consequently, Tom got great experience and exposure to different types and levels of taxes and all parts of the business. Then Dave Chandler left the company, Gary McGrath became controller (in charge of accounting), and Tom became tax manager and then assistant controller in the late 1980s.

After Gary McGrath left in the early 1990s, Tom became treasurer in charge of finance.

When the theaters were sold in 1986, Tom was kept busy preparing spreadsheets but wasn't involved in negotiations. He was, however, involved in the negotiations when the bowls were sold in 1992.

The mergers began by combining units. Then each of the units became a separate company. When a theater was purchased, it would often be incorporated under the name of the theater. Then all those were merged together into Sterling Recreation Organization, Columbia Theater Company, which held the trust properties, and Sterling Theater Co., which held most of the land units. Columbia included Longview and Kelso. SRO had most of the operating assets. In 1993, the three companies were merged together, and Sterling Recreation Organization was renamed Sterling Realty Organization. The mergers were part of a plan to get the company to Subchapter S status and blow up the trusts. By that time, David had been elected president of the company, and Tom was vice president and treasurer. It was during this time that Tom started working more with David, and they both still worked with Fred, usually meeting with him weekly until sometime in 1995, but he was often ill by then.

As officers of the company, David and Tom spent much of their time between 1993 and 1998 dealing with litigation. This five-year odyssey finally culminated in the distribution of the trusts in 1998.

On August 2, 1999, Alison and I assumed our new roles. David and Tom continued to run the company as before with Alison and me joining them on the Senior Management Team. While we worked hard to absorb all the new ideas and information, we both had steep learning curves to climb.

By the time Fred was ready to return to work about six months later, we had succeeded in learning enough to understand the issues and to begin to build credibility among board and staff members that we could do the job. We discussed with Fred the idea that he become chairman emeritus, be involved at whatever level he chose, with Alison and me remaining in the co-chair roles. Fred agreed, and the baton gently passed to the third generation of the Danz family.

Alison retained her Lease Administration position and added the managerial duties to her workload.

When I assumed my new role at SRO, I already had more than thirty years of experience in a variety of organizations. This breadth of experience enabled me to bring to the organization a much different and broader view of organizational structures.

Sterling had always been a traditional top-down operation, a little formal (even Fred's daughter called him "Mr. Danz," men wore suits, and women wore dresses and heels), and for most of its history, very male-dominated. In the entire history of the company, there had only been one woman even close to the top level of management, Marge Turner; manager of the Bowling Division.

Marge Turner, division manager, Bowls Division, with Jerry Vitus.

Part of my effort to understand the company included a study of the existing personnel policies. I found policies that I could only describe as archaic (for example, two weeks of vacation a year for the first four years, three weeks from five to fourteen years of service, and four weeks after fifteen years … and no additional vacation time, no matter how long employment lasted).

Over the next few years, our management team worked to change the policies, which altered the very culture of the company by openly and consistently recognizing the value of every employee from the very beginning of his or her employment with the organization. We enhanced the vacation policy, added paternity leave, adjusted the sick-leave benefit, and included the entire staff in the bonus plan. Employees immediately recognized that the changes made them stakeholders in the company, that what they did in their jobs affected both the profit of the company and what the company paid them. For instance, a manager of one of the mini storage facilities commented that a piece of the late rents she collected belonged to her and she was going to collect as much of it as possible.

We also installed a more flexible work plan that makes it easier for staff to handle family needs and participate in children's activities.

The final issue was the most difficult to solve. We found ourselves facing the fact that most of the twenty employees that worked for SRO had spent all or most of their working lives with the company. One property manager had been with Sterling for more than twenty-five years. Two or three long-time staff members had never worked any place else. All except one had been with the company for more than ten years. We set a goal to find a way for every employee who retired from SRO having spent a significant proportion of their working life at the company to be able to retire with close to the same income as they earned during their active working life. We examined a variety of options, but all were either much too cumbersome, requiring huge amounts of federal and state reporting, or not legal because of some of the rules put in place after the Enron retirement funds scandal. It took a very long time to accomplish, but we put into place a plan that goes a long way towards the goal.

The new majority owners of SRO all had grown children by now. Barbara and her husband, Ted Daniels, had three adult children. Penny Coe had two almost-grown sons. My own son, Jason Horning, worked in the office during the summers through college and then joined the company as a full-time employee in 1996. When the third generation became the owners of the company, Jason was already a property manager, the first of the fourth generation to become significantly involved. Alison's three children were younger and were still at school in 1999.

As the century ended, David Schooler was the president of the company, Alison and I were the co-chairs, Tom Gilchrist was vice president and treasurer, and Fred was chairman emeritus. While Fred was often unwell, he continued to come to the office frequently, kept up on all the issues, spoke with Alison almost daily, and conferred with David by phone when he was not able to come in to the office.

The new millennium began as brightly for SRO as it began for the nation and the region. The federal budget was, for a short time, balanced. The Dot-Com Boom made million- and billionaires out of youngsters who rode the wave of technology into the twenty-first century. Real estate values, residential and commercial, rose dramatically with no end in sight. Financially, 2001 was the best year in SRO history with not only the most profit ever but also the highest ratio of profit to revenue at 42 percent. As a comparison, profits were just 11 percent of revenue during 1986, the last full year of theater, bowling, and radio operations.

At the end of the 1990s, the company still operated two drive-ins and a swap meet, two mini-storage facilities (Arlington and Spokane), and telecommunications facilities in Longmont and Lee Hill, Colorado (west of Boulder), West Seattle, on top of Sterling Plaza in Factoria, and a few other scattered spots.

The major focus of the company became renting land and building space to rent to tenants. As a commercial real estate development and property-management company, the pace changed dramatically. A project now took as long as a decade or more to move from concept to fruition. The company spent time and energy developing more than fourteen properties during this last decade of the century.

All during the late 1950s and into the 1960s, it was very difficult to finance the building of new theaters so John, and later Fred, had to sell land to fund building projects. There was even a time while

David Schooler worked for the City of Bellevue when there was a great deal of excitement because the city was working on a deal that would trade Sterling Recreation property for the site that was the old city hall. (A Lexus dealership is there now.) Fortunately for Sterling, the deal never closed.

A look at the deeds for the downtown Bellevue property, which John originally purchased in 1955, shows that we sold all the parcels along Northeast Eighth during these years. Union Oil Company exercised an option to purchase (for $57,600) the southeast corner of 106th Northeast and Northeast Eighth in March 1958. At the end of that year, SRO sold the next parcel to the east, where the Center Building is located, to the Center Building Company for $42,500. The Center Building Company was owned by Norwood Nickels, Ralph James, a well-known commercial property investor, and an attorney named Howard Tuttle.

The parcel next door, where the building now called Sterling on Eighth is located (known as the Tower Records building for many years) was sold to Eugene Boyd in 1960 for $125,000. Metke Ford had been on the final parcel at the southwest corner of Northeast Eighth and 108th Northeast since 1962. We purchased it again for $497,000 (about $5.00 a foot) in October 1971. That transaction occurred before David came to work at the company, but it was David who leased the land to Platis for a Cadillac dealership. At the time, Jerry Vitus warned him that "if we can't get out of this lease, you're fired." (We would need to terminate the lease in order to develop the corner property.) As usual, David knew what he was doing—the lease had a termination clause.

In the late 1960s, Fred was friendly with people at Winmar, the development arm of Safeco Insurance Company. He leased the section of land on the west side of 106th Northeast at the corner of Northeast Eighth to Winmar to build the office building that is still there. Paccar leased the entire building and then, in 1976, purchased the building from Winmar and the land from SRO in a trade that included two parcels of land in California and a parking lot in Seattle at the northwest corner of Fifth and Lenora. Eventually SRO built theaters on those two California parcels. The Seattle parking lot was used for many years as parking for the Cinerama Theater.

In 2011, the downtown Bellevue property is still one the most valuable pieces in our portfolio. This superblock, which was a berry farm when John Danz purchased it, was reassembled during the last decade or so with the repurchase of the former Tower Records building at 10635 Northeast Eighth (1993), the corner at 106th Northeast and Northeast Eighth (2001), and the Center Building (2006) until SRO finally owned the entire 8.25-acre block—again.

Sterling on 8th, formerly Tower Records Building.

Center Building.

In the middle of the block on 108th Northeast, the building called Key Center, approved by the board of directors in 1990, was ready to open in 1999, having been 90 percent preleased. This building sits on a ninety-nine-year land lease. The most unusual feature of this lease is that the land is unsubordinated. This means that the mortgagee does not have the right to take the land if the mortgage isn't paid. It may be the first lease of its kind for a high-rise office building in Puget Sound.

Key Center.

In 1999, the company sold several properties—the building in Bellevue called the Atrium Building, the parking lot in downtown Seattle, and the Sun Villa Bowl, which was sold to Fred's daughter, Laurie Hamlin. The Sun Villa property was adjacent to the shopping center she had purchased several years earlier, and she was happy to have the several easements between the properties disappear. The proceeds from these sales were used as trade proceeds (a company has a period of time, usually ninety days, in which to identify a property and then another 180 days in which to place the funds into that property or capital gains taxes will apply) to acquire a seventy-five-thousand-square-foot complex of office buildings on six acres called Campus Office Park, located a block north of Overlake Hospital near downtown Bellevue.

Campus Office Park. The two buildings closest to I 405 were taken for a new freeway exit.

The City of Bellevue did a major land use study that resulted in, among other things, a significant rezone of Campus Office Park property that would allow the company to create 135,000 square feet of building on the property. Then in 2008, the State Department of Transportation condemned a portion of the land for use in the creation of a freeway exit, and two of the six buildings fell to the wrecking ball. However, the Land Use Code was changed again so that the company will now be allowed to build an office complex of about two hundred thousand square feet when it is time to redevelop the property.

At a third Bellevue property in Factoria, the new five-story, ninety-three-thousand-square-foot Sterling Plaza II was completed and leased. A company called Stamps.com was originally going to take the entire building, but Stamps sold its Washington business to UPS, which leased only one of the floors and then brought in a division of the Boeing Company to occupy the other four.

Sterling Plaza II.

Moving south, SRO made significant changes at the Lewis & Clark property on Highway 99 during the first half of the decade, building an airport parking lot called Shuttle Park 2. As commercial real estate developers and managers, we had no intention of operating this facility and were able to create an excellent working relationship with an experienced parking facility operator. This eleven-hundred-car airport parking lot was permitted, built, and opened with very positive results, above the estimates of the projections.

Lewis & Clark property and Shuttle Park 2.

In 2001, just prior to declaring bankruptcy, AMF Bowling Centers, which had been leasing and operating the Lewis & Clark Bowling Center, did a midnight move-out of all the bowling equipment, including the lanes. The building remained empty for almost three years during which time, (in 2003) the theater lease expired and was not renewed. In 2004 that we were finally able to sign a lease with Avis to fill both the theater and the bowl space.

From the time David first came to SRO, the company wanted to expand at Lewis & Clark. In 2005, we were able to buy the land and buildings of an adjacent piece that fronts on Highway 99 and includes the El Charro restaurant, an Ace Hardware, and a couple of other small businesses.

Further south, the Tacoma South shopping center saw a major remodel, two new building pads, the addition of the former State Farm parcel, and a new eight-thousand-square-foot building.

As the leases on the theaters expired, the company found other ways to use the buildings. In 2002, Pure Fitness leased the former Tacoma South theater building when the operator decided not to renew the lease. The theater in Portland was torn down and replaced with the GI Joe's retail sport center. The John Danz Theatre became a Good Guys electronics store, then Underhill's Furniture, and today is leased to a church with more than fifteen hundred members. The Liberty Theatre in Walla Walla was gifted by the company to Whitman College.

Going north from Bellevue, when the theater lease in Alderwood ended, the company worked on a plan to redevelop the property, resulting in a lease with Kohls Department Store for a ninety-eight-thousand-square-foot, two-story store, which opened in 2006.

In Lynnwood, for our property that fronts on Highway 99, there was a long negotiation with a big-box store, but it backed out at the beginning of the recession. SRO set out on a program to add as many parcels to the existing space as reasonably possible and has seen quite a bit of success in adding several during the second half of the decade. Once the current recession ends, we anticipate that a shopping-center development will grow in this expanding retail neighborhood. A letter of intent has been signed with a health and fitness center, which we expect will be the first business to open in this new center.

David Schooler believes that the Puget Park Drive-In was the last drive-in theater on I-5 between Canada and California. SRO operated Puget Park as a theater from 1968 through the summer of 2009. A swap started there in 1972 and continued throughout the life of the theater, serving its final customer on October 31, 2009. At that time, SRO agreed to sell fifteen of the twenty-five acres to Swedish Hospital for a new emergency care facility. If all goes as planned, SRO will build a medical office park on the remaining acreage to compliment the clinic.

In 2005, the company sold the Hastings Theatre in Pasadena and used the proceeds to do a like-kind trade for a 107,000-square-foot business park in Mukilteo near Paine Field, renamed Sterling Business Park. The property includes six low-rise buildings leased to a few small manufacturing companies, a variety of business offices, and a few professional services

Sterling Business Park.

Finally, in Bellingham, SRO continues to operate SRO Center, which includes a Ross Dress for Less department store and several small retail shops. Also in Bellingham, the Samish Drive-in Theatre closed in 2001, and the company leased the land to Western Washington University for a parking lot until, in 2007, the university was able to purchase the property.

Ross Dress for Less in the Sterling Center in Bellingham.

Other sales during the decade included a lot on Roosevelt Avenue in the University District of Seattle and both the Island Vue (Longview) and East Sprague (Spokane) drive-in theaters.

In the spring of 2003, SRO took a detour from commercial real estate and partnered with a long time residential apartment owner/operator in the purchase of the Meridian Ridge Apartment complex. We learned a lot about the apartment business and about the character of SRO. Low-end apartment rentals are not a business we want to participate in, and apartment buildings of any kind will probably not be an area of interest any time in the foreseeable future. The complex was sold in 2006.

In the winter of 2004, Barbara's son Will Daniels, the eldest member of the fourth generation, joined the company as a property manager. Within a few years, Barbara left the board of directors ,and Will was elected to the position. Will now serves as the corporate secretary. Then Penny Coe stepped down, and her eldest son, Adrian

Ashkenazy, assumed a board position. Jason Horning served as secretary of SRO for several years and, in that role, also attended all the board meetings. I retired from my role as co-chairwoman in 2008, and Jason and Will both became members of the management team. When I relinquished my board position in 2010, Jason was elected to the board by the stockholders. Alison's third child, Ben, has also joined the company and fills the lease administrator function. While David and Tom still manage the day-to-day operations of the company, the third generation has moved forward with the process of passing family oversight to the fourth generation.

Historically, there has been a rhythm to the commercial real estate market in the Seattle area. Since the 1960s, the industry saw a pattern of ten-year cycles. The first half of each decade reflected a slow down with improving conditions in the second half. This final decade of Sterling's first one hundred years saw that cycle change dramatically. The 2000s opened customarily with the best year ever in the history of SRO and closed with the usual slump. But the decade of the 2010s shows no corresponding upswing, at least immediately. We see concern and belt tightening in the deepest recession since the 1930s. In 2001, SRO had a vacancy rate of 4 percent. In 2006, it dropped to a low of 1.4 percent. In 2009, vacancies shot to a whopping 17 percent.

With conservative and very skilled management in place, the company is well positioned to weather the current recession. There was some belt tightening, and a few plans were postponed, but the mix of office and retail properties and our geographic distribution provide some additional protection.

Fred became less and less involved in the operations of the company during the second half of the decade, spending most of the winter months in Hawaii and, unfortunately, feeling too poorly to participate much of the time when he was home in Kirkland. He died peacefully at Overlake Hospital on August 21, 2009.

The board of Sterling Realty Organization now consists of nine board members. There are four family members: Alison Danz, the sole remaining board member of the third generation of the Danz family, and three members of the fourth generation - Will Daniels, Jason Horning and Adrian Ashkenazy. There are three outside board members and two non-family staff members - David Schooler, the president of the organization, and Tom Gilchrist, the vice president and treasurer. The board has been working on a succession plan for several years as David anticipates that he will remain with the company as president only through 2014, at which time he will most likely assume the position of chairman of the board. Tom Gilchrist has been tagged to move in to the president's office at that time. These changes will give the company excellent continuity as well as maintain the knowledge, expertise, and contacts that have been built up over the past thirty years.

꧁ ꧂

While Sterling Realty Organization bears little similarity to the Sterling Theatre company built by John Danz in the early twentieth century, there are similarities in the things that many might consider most important. It makes no difference whether one is selling theater tickets and popcorn or negotiating a multi-year multi-million-dollar lease in the values the company expects of every employee. The company has a culture of excellence instilled into its very fabric. Each employee from company president to accounting staff to property manager to maintenance staff is expected to deal with every tenant in every building as if he or she were the most important tenant in the company. Service, honesty, a fair deal, and reasonable accommodations are the norm, not the exception. Like John, those responsible for running the company feel that each employee represents them, and the four of us who are the majority owners also think that each employee represents each of us in the community. This is a company that we can be proud to be associated with and which I, personally, would be even prouder to see move strongly into the fourth and fifth generations of management and ownership.

꧁ ꧂

In my research for this story, I came across a letter to my grandfather with a message I would like to leave to the fourth and fifth generations.

Back in 1952, John turned seventy-five and threw himself a birthday party, inviting friends, family members, and many business associates to a "men only" party. Philip Schaeffer of West and Wheeler real estate wrote to John, calling him his company's most valued client, noting that John had purchased the Class A Theatre building, the Winter Garden Theatre, the Commodore apartment house, the Savoy Hotel, and other properties from them. He mentioned John's speech at the party in which he regarded his real start in the picture business on a large scale to be the Capitol Theatre (purchased in 1919). Schaeffer wrote, "To many of your friends it seemed venturesome on your part to have a picture theatre there, however, you fooled them all and came up smiling, your word was as good as a bond, and has always been that way as long as I have known you." Schaeffer was reminded of a sentiment that he had copied from a pillar on John Wanamaker's store in Philadelphia.

> Let those who follow me to continue to build with the plumb of honor, the level of truth and the square of integrity, education, courtesy and mutuality.

—

Corporate Snapshot 1950s			
Corporation	**Inc**	**Acq**	**Holding**
Acme Theatre Company	1918	1918	Florence, Circle Property, University Property, Lynn Theatre (operate)
Admiral Theatre Company	1942	1942	Admiral
Capitol Amusement Company	1924	1924	Palomar, Garden, Hi-Line (operate), Lewis & Clark Bowl
Columbia Theatre Company	1924	1945	Columbia (Longview)
Comet Theatre Enterprises	1949	1949	Hastings, Covina (CA)
Covina Drive In Theatre Corporation	1959	1959	Covina Drive-In (CA)
Cowlitz Amusements	1928	1942	Kelso
Elwha Theatre	1931	1953	Elwha
Farwest Theatres	1930	1930	Arabian, Mission, Uptown; Merged with Sterling Co., Inc., 1954
Globe Amusement Company	1917	1917	Colonial, Music Box

Corporate Snapshot 1950s			
Corporation	**Inc**	**Acq**	**Holding**
Granada Theatre Company	1926	1926	Granada
La Mirada Company	1942	1942	La Mirada Drive-In (CA)
Mathews-Moran Amusement Company	1928	1936	Norwalk (CA), The Dalles (OR), Blue Mouse
Northwestern Theatrical Enterprises	1926	1933 ?	Roosevelt Theatre; Merged with Admiral Theatre Company, 1953
Oak Theatre	1922	1930	Magnolia, Sunset Drive-In, lease on Rivoli; Merged with Sterling Co., Inc., 1954
The Progressive Company	1920	1920	Lewis & Clark Property, Tacoma Land (Newman Land); Merged with Portola, 1943
Rainier Theatre Company	1923	1923	Commodore-Duchess Apartments, John Danz Theatre, Island Vue Drive-In
Sterling Management Company	1965	1965	Corporate Management

Corporate Snapshot 1950s			
Corporation	**Inc**	**Acq**	**Holding**
Sterling Men's Wear Company	1915	1915	Colonial, Florence, Grove Theatre (CA) Operations, Belle Lanes Bowl, Belle Lanes Operations
Sterling Realty Company	1955	1955	(Holding property only) Belle Lanes, Hi-Line Theatre (Operate), Lake City, Lynnwood Holding, Lynn Theatre
Sterling Theatres	1927	1927	Neptune, Northgate Theatre, Palomar Building, Queen Anne Bowl; Merged with Sterling Theatre Company,1954
Third & University Corporation	1936	1936	Garden Property
Vision Corporation	Do not know	1942	Longview
Whatcom Management Company	1968	1968	KBFW, KENY (Bellingham)
Your Drive-In Theatre, Inc.	1950	1950	Your Drive-In (Longview)

Corporate Snapshot 1986		
Asset	Type	Location
Bellevue Office	Office	Bellevue, WA
Bellevue Shop	Shop - Lease	Bellevue, WA
Tri-Cities Office	Office	Kennewick, WA
California Office	Office - Lease	West Hollywood, CA
Spokane Office	Office	Spokane, WA
Admiral Theatre	Theater & Land	Seattle, WA
Capri Theatre	Theater & Land	West Covina, CA
Cinerama Theatre	Ground Lease	Seattle, WA
Clearwater Cinemas	Theater & Land	Spokane, WA
Columbia Center	Theater & Land	Kennewick, WA
Factoria	Theater & Land	Bellevue, WA
Garland Theatre	Theater & Land	Spokane, WA
Gateway Theatre	Theater & Land	La Mirada, CA
Grand Cinemas	Theater & Land	Alderwood, WA
John Danz Theater	Theater & Land	Bellevue, WA
Kirkland Park Place	Lease	Kirkland, WA

Corporate Snapshot 1986		
Asset	**Type**	**Location**
Lake City Theatre	Theatre & Land	Lake City, WA
Lewis & Clark	Theater, Bowling Center, Land	Tukwila, WA
Liberty Theatre	Theater and Land	Walla Walla, WA
Lincoln Heights	Lease	Spokane, WA
Longview Theatre	Theater and Land	Longview, WA
Lynn Theatre	Theater and Land	Lynnwood, WA
Lyons Avenue Cinemas	Lease	Spokane, WA
Metro Theatre	Lease	Kennewick, WA
Montclair Theater	Theater Building and Land	Montclair, CA
Mount Baker Theatre	Lease	Bellingham, WA
Northgate Theatre	Ground Lease	Seattle, WA
Oak Tree Village	Leasehold	Seattle, WA
Pasadena Hastings Theatre	Theater and Land	Pasadena, CA
Pasco Theatre	Theater and Land	Pasco, WA
Riverpark Theater	Lease	Spokane, WA
Sehome Theatre	Theater and Land	Bellingham, WA

Corporate Snapshot 1986		
Asset	**Type**	**Location**
Southcenter	Ground Lease	Tukwila, WA
State Theater	Theater and Land	Spokane, WA
Tacoma Mall Theater	Ground Lease	Tacoma, WA
Tacoma South Theatre	Theater and Land	Tacoma, WA
Tacoma West Theater	Lease	Tacoma, WA
Totem Lake Cinemas	Ground Lease	Kirkland, WA
Triangle Cinemas	Theatre and Land	Longview, WA
Uptown Theatre	Theater and Land	Richland, WA
Uptown Theatre	Ground Lease	Seattle, WA
Viking Twin Theater	Theater and Land	Spokane, WA
Bel-Kirk Drive-In	Lease	Kirkland, WA
Eastside Drive-In	Lease	Kirkland, WA
East Sprague Drive-In	Drive-in Theater, Land	Spokane, WA
East Trent Drive-In	Drive-in Theater, Land	Spokane, WA
Indio Drive-In	Drive-in Theater, Land	Indio, CA

Corporate Snapshot 1986		
Asset	**Type**	**Location**
Island View Drive-In	Drive-in Theater, Land	Kennewick, WA
Kelso Drive-In	Drive-in Theater, Land	Kelso, WA
North Cedar Drive-In	Drive-in Theater and Land	Spokane
Puget Park Drive-In & Swap	Drive-in Theater & Swap Meet, Land	Everett, WA
River View Drive-In & Swap	Drive-in Theater & Swap Meet, Land	Pasco, WA
Samish Drive-In	Drive-in Theater and Land	Bellingham, WA
Sky-vue Drive-In	Drive-in Theater and Land	Walla Walla, WA
West End Drive-In	Drive in Theater and Land	Spokane, WA
Your Drive-In	Drive in Theater and Land	Longview, WA
20th Century Bowl	Bowl, Grill, Lounge – Lease	Portland, OR
Belle Lanes Bowl	Bowl, Grill, Land	Bellevue, WA
Gateway Bowl	Bowl, Grill, Subtenant - Lease	Portland, OR
Sportsworld Bowl	Bowl, Grill, Pull Tabs, Lounge – Lease	Federal Way, WA

Corporate Snapshot 1986		
Asset	**Type**	**Location**
Sun Villa Bowl	Bowl, Grill, Lounge, Land	Bellevue, WA
Westpark Bowl	Bowl, Grill, Pull Tabs, Lounge - Lease	Bremerton, WA
Tacoma South Shopping Center	Buildings and Land	Tacoma, WA
KALE-KIOK	AM/FM Radio Station	Kennewick, WA
KZOK-KJET	AM/FM Radio Station	Seattle, WA
KDKO Transmitter	Land	Denver, CO
Denver/Boulder Radio Stations	Radio Stations	Colorado
Las Vegas Radio Station	Radio Station	Nevada
Racine Radio Stations	Radio Stations	Wisconsin
Ad Agency West	Advertising Agency	Bellevue, WA
Amusement Devices	Arcade Machines	Bellevue, WA
Bakersfield Land	Land	Bakersfield, CA
Benton Theatre Property	Theater and Land	Kennewick, WA

Corporate Snapshot 1986		
Asset	**Type**	**Location**
California Condo	Condominium	Los Angeles. CA
Chatfield House	House and Land	Denver, CO
Cinerama Lot	Parking Lot	Seattle, WA
Colorado Land	FM Transmitter Site and Land	Colorado
Columbia Leasing	Leasing Agency	Kennewick, WA
Jefferson Land	Land	Walla Walla, WA
Ken-Cade Building	Office Building	Kennewick, WA
Kennewick House	House and Land	Kennewick, WA
Metke Land	Land	Bellevue, WA
Maple Valley Land	Land	Maple Valley, WA
Redmond Land	Land	Redmond, WA
Roosevelt land	Parking lot	Seattle, WA
Vista Way House	House and Land	Kelso, WA

ABOUT THE AUTHORS

Carolee Danz, a Seattle native, worked in the motion picture and television industry before earning a Master of Social Work degree from the University of Washington. She then worked as a professional fund raiser for various non-profit organizations for twenty years. Now retired, she resides in Kirkland, Washington and spends many months a year exploring the world.

❧ ❧

David Wilma has authored and co-authored four books and a video documentary on Pacific Northwest history. His history essays appear at www.HistoryLink.org, the free online encyclopedia of Washington State history.